I0794461

Praise for
PSALMS

"God's people need guidance for their prayer lives, and the Psalms are a rich resource. Holloway helps us explore the Psalms as a guide for lament, thanksgiving, praise, and celebration. I enthusiastically recommend his book, especially for small groups and spiritual formation retreats."

—**Sara G. Barton,** Pepperdine University Chaplain

"In the current hostile climate of racial and political division, Gary Holloway's Meditative Commentary on Psalms comes as a much needed gift to the fragmented church in America. Holloway approaches the Psalms by using the spiritual practice of *Lectio Divina*. He skillfully uses this method to transfer God's Word written on ancient tablets of stones to the written Word on living hearts made of flesh. This is an excellent resource for spiritual retreats designed to foster spiritual growth and spiritual intimacy in building community across the divisive lines of politics and race."

—**Dr. Jerry Andrew Taylor,** Associate Professor of Bible, Missions, and Ministry, Abilene Christian University; Founding Director of the Carl Spain Center on Race Studies and Spiritual Action

"*Psalms: Hymns of God's People* reminds me of C. S. Lewis's *Reflection on the Psalms*, which is one of my favorite devotional books. The goal of deeper Bible study is to make a connection with the source of spirituality—God himself. On our journey to deeper meditation on Scripture, we need a guide who will illuminate the path to spiritual insight. Dr. Holloway is a gracious guide on this journey. This Meditative Commentary both shines a light on the path to God through the Psalms and allows readers to discover the path and make it their own."

—**Dr. G. Steve Kinnard,** Editor of *Teleios*; Adjunct Professor of New Testament, Lincoln Christian University; Professor of Bible/Dean of Ministry and Bible, Rocky Mountain School of Ministry and Theology

"I love a book that makes me think, and then makes me think of who I want to share it with. I want to share this book with you! In *Psalms: Hymns of God's People*, Gary Holloway cracks the code of meaningful meditation. His astute scholarship and engaging style inspire and equip. Whether you're new to the Bible or have spent your life poring over its pages, you will find yourself hearing God's life-giving voice in fresh ways and thinking of who you want to share it with."

—**Dr. Don McLaughlin,** author of *Love First: Ending Hate before It's Too Late*

"Gary Holloway is a master of simple prose that gets to the heart of things and draws readers in. Here he has applied that skill to produce a rich but simple tool to make the Psalms—the believer's prayerbook—a regular part of one's life with God."

—**Leonard Allen,** author of *Poured Out: The Spirit of God Empowering the Mission of God*

A MEDITATIVE COMMENTARY
on the Old Testament

PSALMS

HYMNS OF GOD'S PEOPLE

A MEDITATIVE COMMENTARY
on the Old Testament

PSALMS

HYMNS OF GOD'S PEOPLE

GARY HOLLOWAY

LEAFWOOD
PUBLISHERS
an imprint of Abilene Christian University Press

PSALMS

HYMNS OF GOD'S PEOPLE

A Meditative Commentary

LEAFWOOD PUBLISHERS

an imprint of Abilene Christian University Press

ISBN 978-1-68426-261-8 | LCCN 2021049078

Printed in the United States of America

LIBRARY OF CONGRESS CATALOGING-IN-PUBLICATION DATA
Names: Holloway, Gary, 1956- author.
Title: Psalms : hymns of God's people / Gary Holloway.
Other titles: Hymns of God's people
Description: Abilene, Tex. : Leafwood Publishers, 2022.
Identifiers: LCCN 2021049078 (print) | LCCN 2021049079 (ebook) | ISBN 9781684262618 (paperback) | ISBN 9781684268900 (ebook)
Subjects: LCSH: Bible. Psalms—Criticism, interpretation, etc.
Classification: LCC BS1430.52 .H65 2022 (print) | LCC BS1430.52 (ebook) | DDC 223.2—dc23
LC record available at https://lccn.loc.gov/2021049078
LC ebook record available at https://lccn.loc.gov/2021049079

Cover design by Bruce Gore
Interior text design by Sandy Armstrong, Strong Design

Leafwood Publishers is an imprint of Abilene Christian University Press
For information contact:
ACU Box 29138
Abilene, Texas 79699

1-877-816-4455
www.leafwoodpublishers.com

22 23 24 25 26 27 28 / 7 6 5 4 3 2 1

To the Vultee Church of Christ

CONTENTS

INTRODUCTION

HEARING GOD IN SCRIPTURE

There are many commentaries, guides, and workbooks on the various books of the Bible. How is this series different? It is not intended to answer all your scholarly questions about the Bible or even make you an expert in the details of Scripture. Instead, this series is designed to help you hear the voice of God in your everyday life. It is a guide to meditation on the Bible—meditation that will allow the Bible to transform you.

We read in many ways. We might scan a newspaper for information, read a map for our location, read a novel for pleasure, or read a textbook to pass a test. These are all good ways to read, depending on our circumstances.

A young soldier far away from home who receives a letter from his wife reads in yet another way. He might scan the letter quickly at first for news and information. But his longing for his beloved causes him to read the letter again and again, hearing her sweet voice in every line. He slowly treasures each word of this precious letter.

In a similar way, there are many good ways to read the Bible, depending on our circumstances. Bible study is absolutely necessary for our life with God. We rightly study the Bible for information. We ask, Who wrote this? When was it written? Who were the original readers? How do these words apply to me? More importantly, we want information about God. Who is he? What does he think of me? What does he want from me?

There is no substitute for this kind of close, dedicated Bible study. We must know what the Bible says to know our standing with God. We therefore read the Bible to discover true doctrine or teaching. But some, in their emphasis on the authority and inspiration of the Bible, have forgotten that Bible study is not an end in itself. We want to know God through Scripture. We want to have a relationship with the Teacher, not just the teachings.

Jesus tells some of God's people in his day, "You study the Scriptures diligently because you think that in them you have eternal life. These are the very Scriptures that testify about me, yet you refuse to come to me to have life" (John 5:39–40 NIV). He's not telling them to study their Bibles less; he is reminding them of the deeper purpose of Bible study—to draw us to God through Jesus. Bible study is a means, not an end.

Yet the way many of us have learned to study the Bible may actually get in the way of hearing God. "Bible study" may sound a lot like schoolwork, and many of us were happy to get out of school. "Bible study" may call to mind pictures of intellectuals surrounded by books in Greek and Hebrew, pondering meanings too deep for ordinary people. The method of Bible study that has been popular for some time focuses on the strangeness of the Bible. It was written long ago, far away, and in languages we cannot read. There is a huge gap between us and the original readers of the Bible—a gap that can only be bridged by scholars, not by average folks.

There is some truth and some value in this "scholarly" method. It is true that the Bible was not written originally to us. Knowing ancient languages and customs can at times help us understand the Bible better. However, one unintended result of this approach is that it forms a distance between the Bible and the people of God. We may come to think that we can only hear God indirectly through Scripture, that his Word must be filtered through scholars. We may even think that deep Bible study is a matter of mastering obscure information about the Bible.

Meditation

We read the Bible for more than information. By studying it, we experience transformation, the mysterious process of God at work in us. Through his loving words, God is calling us to life with him. He is forming us into the image of his Son.

Reading the Bible is not like reading other books. We are not simply trying to learn information or master material. Instead, we want to stand under the authority of Scripture and let God master us. While we read the Bible, it reads us, opening the depths of our being to the overpowering love of God. "For the word of God is alive and active. Sharper than any double-edged sword, it penetrates even to dividing soul and spirit, joints and marrow; it judges the thoughts and attitudes of the heart. Nothing in all creation is hidden from God's sight. Everything is uncovered and laid bare before the eyes of him to whom we must give account" (Heb. 4:12–13 NIV).

Opening our hearts to the Word of God is meditation. Although this way of reading the Bible may be new to some, it has a long heritage among God's people. The Psalmist joyously meditates on the words of God (Ps. 1:2; 39:3; 119:15, 23, 27, 48, 78, 97, 99, 148). Meditation is taking the words of Scripture to heart and letting them ask questions of us. It is slowing down, chewing over a text, listening closely, reading God's message of love to us over and over. This is not a simple, easy, or naïve reading of Scripture, but a process that takes time, dedication, and practice on our part.

There are many ways to meditate on the Bible. One is praying the Scriptures. Prayer and Bible study cannot be separated. One way of praying the Bible is to make the words of a text your prayer. Obviously, the prayer texts of Scripture, especially the Psalms, lend themselves to this. "The LORD is my shepherd" (of Psalm 23) has been the prayer of many hearts.

However, it is proper and helpful to turn the words of the Bible into prayers. Commands from God can become prayers. "You shall have no other gods before me" (Exod. 20:3 NIV) can be prayed: "Lord, keep me from anything that takes your place in my heart." Stories can be prayed. Jesus heals a man born blind (John 9), and so we pray, "Lord Jesus, open my eyes to who you truly are." Even the promises of the Bible become prayers. "Never will I leave you; never will I forsake you" (Deut. 31:6; Heb. 13:5 NIV) becomes "God, help me know your promise that you are always with me so I may live my life without fear."

Obviously, there are many helpful ways of hearing the voice of God in Scripture. Again, the purpose of Bible reading and study is not to know more about the Bible, much less to pride ourselves as experts on Scripture. Instead, we read to hear the voice of our Beloved. We listen for a word of God for us.

Holy Reading

This commentary reflects an ancient way of meditation and praying the Scriptures known as *lectio divina*, or holy reading. This method assumes God wants to speak to us directly in the Bible, that the passage we are reading is God's Word to us right now. The writers of the New Testament read the Old Testament with this same conviction. They saw the words of the Bible speaking directly to their own situation. They read with humility and with prayer.

The first step along this way of holy reading is listening to the Bible. Choose a biblical text that is not too long. This commentary breaks most Psalms into smaller sections intentionally. The purpose is to hear God's voice in your current situation, not to cover material or prepare lessons. It is helpful to hear Scripture in various translations. The passages in this commentary alternate between the New International Version and the New Living Translation. Get into a comfortable position and maintain silence before God for several minutes. This prepares the heart to listen. Read slowly. Savor each word. Perhaps read aloud. Listen for a particular phrase that speaks to you. Ask God, "What are you trying to tell me today?"

The next step is to meditate on that phrase. That meditation may include slowly repeating the phrase that seems to be for you today. As you think deeply on it, you might even memorize it. Committing biblical passages to memory allows us to hold them in our hearts all day long. If you keep a journal, you might write the passage there. Let those words sink deeply into your heart.

Then pray those words back to God in your heart. Those words may call up visual images, smells, sounds, and feelings. Pay attention to what God is giving you in those words. Then respond in faith to what those words say to your heart. What do they call you to be and to do? Our humble response might take the form of praise, thanksgiving, joy, confession, or even cries of pain.

The final step in this "holy reading" is the contemplation of God. The words from God that we receive deeply in our hearts lead us to him. Through these words, we experience union with the all-powerful God of love. Again, one should not separate Bible reading from prayer. The words of God in Scripture transport us into the very presence of God where we joyfully rest in his love.

What keeps us from reading our own desires back into Scripture? How do we know it is God's voice we hear and not our own?

Two things. One is prayer. We are asking God to open our hearts, minds, and lives to him. We ask to hear his voice, not ours and not the voice of the world around us.

The second thing that keeps this from being an exercise in self-deception is to study the Bible in community. By praying over Scripture in a group, we hear God's Word together. God speaks through the other members of our group. The wisdom he gives them keeps us from private, selfish, and unusual interpretations. They help us keep our own voices in check as we desire to listen only to God.

How to Use This Commentary

This commentary assists us in holy reading of the Bible. It gives structure to daily personal devotions, family meditation, small group Bible studies, and church classes.

Daily Devotional

Listening, meditation, prayer, contemplation. How does this commentary fit into this way of Bible study? Consider it as a conversation partner. We have taken a section of Scripture and then broken it down into four short daily readings. After listening, meditating, praying, and contemplating the passage for the day, use the questions suggested in the commentary to provoke deeper reflection. This provides a structure for a daily fifteen-minute devotional four days a week. On the fifth day, read the entire passage, meditate, and then use the questions to reflect on the meaning of the whole scripture. On day six, explore a series of meditations on the passage, which you can treat like a conversation with another who has prayed over the text.

If you want to begin daily Bible reading but need guidance, this provides a Monday through Saturday experience that prepares the heart for worship and praise on Sunday. This structure also results in a communal reading of Scripture, instead of a private reading. Even if you use this commentary alone, you are not reading privately. God is at work in you and in the conversation you have with another (the author of the commentary) who has sought to hear God through this passage of the Bible.

Family Bible Study

This commentary can also provide a space for family Bible study. Many Christian parents want to lead their children in daily study but don't know where to begin or how to structure their time. Using the six-day plan outlined herein means the entire family can read, meditate, pray, and reflect on these short passages, using the questions provided. On day five, your family can review the entire passage, and then on day six, you can read the meditations in the commentary to prompt reflection and discussion. God will bless our families beyond what we once thought possible through our prayerful study of his Word.

Weekly Group Study

This commentary can also structure small group Bible study. Each member of the group should have meditated over the daily readings and questions for the five days preceding the group meeting, using the method outlined herein. The day before the group meeting, each member should read and reflect on the meditations in the commentary on that passage. You then can meet once a week to hear God's Word together. In that group meeting, the method of holy reading would look something like this:

Listening

1. Five minutes of silence
2. Slow reading of the biblical passage for that week
3. A minute of silent meditation on the passage
4. Briefly sharing with the group the word or phrase that struck you

Personal Message

5. A second reading of the same passage
6. A minute of silence
7. Where does this touch your life today?
8. Responses: I hear, I see, etc.

Life Response

9. Brief silence
10. What does God want you to do today in light of this word?

Group Prayer

11. Have each member of the group pray aloud for the person on his or her left, asking God to bless the word he has given them.

The procedure suggested here can be used in churches or neighborhood Bible studies. Church members would use the daily readings Monday to Friday in their daily devotionals. This commentary intentionally provides no readings on the sixth day so we can spend Saturdays as a time of rest—not rest from Bible study, but a time to let God's Word quietly work its way deep into our hearts. Sunday during Bible school or in home meetings, the group would gather to experience the weekly readings together, using the group method described herein. It might be that the sermon for each Sunday could be on the passage for that week.

Some churches have used this structure to great advantage. In the hallways of those church buildings, the talk is not of the local football team or the weather, but of the shared experience of the Word of God for that week. And that is the purpose of our personal and communal study—to hear the voice of God, our loving Father who wants us to love him in return. He deeply desires a personal relationship with us. Father, Son, and Spirit make a home inside us (see John 14:16–17, 23). Our loving God speaks to his children! But we must listen for his voice. That listening is not a matter of gritting our teeth and trying harder to hear. Instead, it is part of our entire life with God. That is what Bible study is all about.

Through daily personal prayer and meditation on God's Word and through a communal reading of Scripture, our most important conversation partner, the Holy Spirit, will do mysterious and marvelous work. Among other things, the Spirit pours God's love into our hearts (Rom. 5:5), bears witness to our spirits that we are God's children (Rom. 8:16), intercedes for us with God (Rom. 8:26), and enlightens us as to God's will (Eph. 1:17).

So this is an invitation to personal daily Bible study, to praying the Scriptures, to sharing with fellow believers, to hearing the voice of God. God will bless us, our families, our churches, and his world if we take the time to be still, listen, and do his word.

THE SPIRITUALITY OF PSALMS

Perhaps, like me, you did not grow up enjoying the Psalms. As a young Christian, I was taught to read through the Bible from Genesis to Revelation. But when I got to the Psalms, the "chapters" did not make sense. Psalm 1 did not logically lead to Psalm 2. There was no sequence to the reading. Moreover, there was little doctrine and instruction in the Psalms. Indeed, they sounded more like human words to God than like God's words to us.

It wasn't until later that I realized the nature of the Psalms. They are human words to God, but no less inspired than the rest of the Bible. The Psalms are heartfelt prayers to God. What's more, they are poetry. Hebrew poetry is not like English poetry. It seldom relies on rhyme or rhythm. Instead, Hebrew poetry is based on parallel thoughts or feelings. In other words, genuine religious emotion is expressed in different words in the lines of the Psalms. Sometimes the feelings are similar in the next line, sometimes opposite, sometimes complementary.

This means the Psalms are poetry put to music. As poetry, the Psalms contain metaphors, exaggeration, and other figurative and expressive language. That's why we find so little that is doctrinal (as we usually define it) in the Psalms. Of course, the Psalms are doctrinal in that they teach, but they teach as poetical prayers. Prayer may have doctrinal implications, but we rarely express doctrine in prayer. Instead, we open our hearts to God in strong emotive language.

The Psalms are thus most like a hymnbook. Reading through the Psalms in order, trying to find a common theme, is like singing through the hymnbook in numerical order, expecting one hymn to naturally lead to another. It does not work that way. Instead we chose hymns and Psalms that best express what we feel at the moment. Thus the best way to pray the Psalms is to begin with the question, "How do I feel toward God at the moment?" then find a Psalm that best expresses that meaning.

We can summarize the types of Psalms this way:

Praying Psalms of Sorrow and Joy

Laments: expressing disappointment, sorrow, struggles (Psalms 3, 12, 22, 31, 39, 42, 44, 51, 57, 71, 80, 94, 120, 137, 139, 142)

Thanksgiving Psalms (Psalms 18, 30, 32, 34, 40, 65, 66, 67, 75, 92, 107, 116, 118, 124, 138)

Hymns of praise (Psalms 8, 19, 33, 66, 100, 103, 104, 111, 113, 114, 117, 145, 146, 147, 148, 149)

Praying Psalms of Affirmation and Celebration

Covenant renewal (Psalms 50, 81)

Royal Psalms (Psalms 2, 20, 21, 45, 72, 101, 110, 144)

Enthronement Psalms (Psalms 24, 29, 47, 93, 95–99)

Songs of Zion and Jerusalem (Psalms 46, 48, 76, 84, 87, 122)

Praying Other Psalms

Salvation history Psalms (Psalms 78, 105, 106, 135, 136)

Wisdom Psalms (Psalms 36, 37, 49, 73, 112, 127, 128, 133)

Songs of trust (Psalms 11, 16, 23, 27, 62, 63, 91, 121, 125, 131)

Note that this book will not look at every Psalm. You may not find a meditation here on your favorite one. But you will be led to meditate on each of these types of Psalms. Using that method, you can then apply it to others of that same type.

So you may go through the meditations in this book in order. Or you may find it more helpful to ask yourself, "How am I feeling today? Do I need to lament? Praise? Give thanks? Remember what God has done in the past?" Then choose the appropriate Psalm on which to meditate. And since the Psalms are songs, at the end of every meditation there will be suggestions of traditional hymns and more contemporary praise songs that you might wish to sing.

But, like the Psalm writers, we do not pray alone. We pray with God's covenant people. The Psalmists lifted up God's people, Israel, in prayer. We also pray for God's people and for God's world. Like the Psalmist, we live in a world of injustice. In the face of poverty, racism, violence, and war, the Psalms give us words to plead for justice. We pray and sing in solidarity with the oppressed.

And we also sing and pray with Jesus. When Christians end their prayers with "In Jesus's name," we are not merely signing off on the prayer. Jesus is there with us and in us, bringing our cries to the Father. The Old Testament book that is quoted most often in the New Testament is Psalms. That's because the earliest Christians heard these hymns as more than the cry of Israel. They are also the songs of the Messiah, the one who embodies Israel.

This helps us pray the Psalms as Christians. If we cannot imagine being surrounded by enemies, we do know that Jesus was surrounded. If we do not feel abandoned by God, we know that Jesus felt that way. If we have trouble believing that God will bring justice and make all things right, we can hear the voice of the faithful Jesus in us, the one who trusted the Father, even on the cross.

As we meditate on the Psalms, we sing and pray from the heart. We sing and pray with God's people. We sing and pray for the oppressed. We sing and pray with Jesus and the Spirit.

MEDITATIONS

PART ONE

PRAYING PSALMS OF SORROW AND JOY

LAMENTS

As I write these words, we are in the midst of the worst part of the coronavirus pandemic. The economy has tanked. Some supplies are scarce. We are practicing social distancing. Many have lost their jobs and do not know how they will provide for their families. Some are sick and dying.

We are isolated, lonely, and afraid. We have not been able to meet with fellow Christians face-to-face for months. We do not know when or how this will end.

And we wonder what God is doing. Where is he? Has he abandoned us?

If you are reading this long after the pandemic, you may wonder at our lack of faith. Looking back, it may be clear that everything worked out and we returned to normal. But there are always challenges in life, always enemies—war, hunger, depression, violence, despair.

In the face of all this, we need words to express the deepest anguish of our hearts. Psalms provide that language—the language of lament. In these biblical laments, God's faithful ones honestly pour out their grief to him. Some of us have been taught (erroneously) to hide our feelings and put on a happy face before God. But we cannot hide from him. And we should not. He is our loving Father who is able to take our anger and disappointment.

So as we meditate on these lament Psalms, we do so as those who trust in God especially when it seems there is no reason to trust. You will notice a pattern in these laments. They usually begin with shockingly honest complaints against God. They continue with reminders of how God has faithfully blessed us in the past. And they end with trust in God. In times of deep trouble when we are desperate, we use these Psalms to faithfully lament.

LAMENTS OVER FOES

Psalms 3 and 142

DAY ONE READING AND QUESTIONS

Psalm 3 (NIV)

LORD, how many are my foes!
  How many rise up against me!
Many are saying of me,
  "God will not deliver him."
But you, LORD, are a shield around me,
  my glory, the One who lifts my head high.
I call out to the LORD,
  and he answers me from his holy mountain.

1. *Should a Christian have enemies? Do you have foes (enemies)? Can you see the faces of those who are against you?*

2. *Has anyone ever ridiculed your faith? Do they look at you and think God has abandoned you? How does that make you feel?*

3. *How does God shield us? What does it mean to "lift the head"? Are you hanging your head?*

DAY TWO READING AND QUESTIONS

Psalm 3 (NIV)

I lie down and sleep;
  I wake again, because the LORD sustains me.
I will not fear though tens of thousands
  assail me on every side.

Arise, LORD!
    Deliver me, my God!
Strike all my enemies on the jaw;
    break the teeth of the wicked.
From the LORD comes deliverance.
    May your blessing be on your people.

1. *Do you have trouble sleeping? Do you dread getting up in the morning? Why? How can God help us sleep and wake?*

2. *Do you ever want to punch someone in the mouth? Should we ask God to punch them for us?*

3. *This Psalm asks for God's blessing on "your people." How can we lament together?*

DAY THREE READING AND QUESTIONS

Psalm 142 (NLT)

I cry out to the LORD;
    I plead for the LORD's mercy.
I pour out my complaints before him
    and tell him all my troubles.
When I am overwhelmed,
    you alone know the way I should turn.
Wherever I go,
    my enemies have set traps for me.
I look for someone to come and help me,
    but no one gives me a passing thought!
No one will help me;
    no one cares a bit what happens to me.

1. *Should we complain to God? Is there a time we should not complain?*

2. *Has anyone ever "set a trap" for you? Think of times when those you trust have stabbed you in the back. How did that make you feel?*

3. *"No one cares a bit what happens to me." Is this whining? Or do we honestly feel this way at times? Should we feel this way?*

DAY FOUR READING AND QUESTIONS

Psalm 142 (NLT)

Then I pray to you, O Lord.
    I say, "You are my place of refuge.
    You are all I really want in life.
Hear my cry,
    for I am very low.
Rescue me from my persecutors,
    for they are too strong for me.
Bring me out of prison
    so I can thank you.
The godly will crowd around me,
    for you are good to me."

1. *What is a refuge? Why do we need one?*

2. *Are we usually desperate enough to come to God, or do we usually think we can handle things on our own? Do we need more desperation?*

3. *How can lament end in praise? Why will the righteous gather around faithful lamenters?*

DAY FIVE READING AND QUESTIONS

Go back and read Psalms 3 and 142.

1. *What do we lose when we refuse to admit we have enemies? What do we lose by refusing to complain to God?*

2. *Doesn't every honest relationship sometimes demand complaint?*

3. *How are these two Psalms "faithful" laments?*

Meditation on Psalms 3 and 142

Jesus said to love your enemies. But many of us have been taught that we should have no enemies. We should make everyone our friend. Or at least pretend they are.

But Jesus had enemies. They lied about him, plotted against him, and put him on a cross. And still he said, "Father, forgive them."

How can we love our enemies unless we first admit we have them?

So how do we treat our enemies? "Love them," Jesus says. But how do we do that? Loving our enemies means we want them to turn to God and be forgiven. No sin is beyond his mercy. But it does not mean we want them to get away with it. Forgiveness is not permission to harm us or to harm anyone else. These actions demand repayment. They demand justice, even (properly understood) vengeance.

These Psalms give us language to admit we have enemies. How our foes surround us! And these Psalms show us how to handle our enemies. We bring them to God. We might want to sock them in the face and knock their teeth down their throats. But we do not. We trust God to deal with them. "Vengeance is mine," says the Lord (Rom. 12:19 KJV). We do not take vengeance into our own hands.

So we take our complaints to God. Many of us have been taught that we should never complain to God. But the Psalmist does. And Jesus did (using the words of a Psalm): "My God, my God, why have you forsaken me?" (Matt. 27:46; Ps. 22:1 NIV). Complaining to God can be mere selfish whining. But honest complaints are part of a genuine relationship. When trouble comes, we are honest with God. We cry. He hears. He acts. We praise his name with the righteous.

"Lord, deliver us from our foes this day! May we always bring our honest complaints to you, knowing that you hear."

Consider singing these songs as you continue your meditation: "Amazing Grace" and "I Will Call Upon the Lord."

LAMENTS WHEN FORSAKEN

Psalms 22 and 42

DAY ONE READING AND QUESTIONS

Psalm 22 (NIV)

My God, my God, why have you forsaken me?
    Why are you so far from saving me,
    so far from my cries of anguish?
My God, I cry out by day, but you do not answer,
    by night, but I find no rest.
Yet you are enthroned as the Holy One;
    you are the one Israel praises.
In you our ancestors put their trust;
    they trusted and you delivered them.
To you they cried out and were saved;
    in you they trusted and were not put to shame.
But I am a worm and not a man,
    scorned by everyone, despised by the people.
All who see me mock me;
    they hurl insults, shaking their heads.
"He trusts in the LORD," they say,
    "let the LORD rescue him.
Let him deliver him,
    since he delights in him."
Yet you brought me out of the womb;
    you made me trust in you, even at my mother's breast.
From birth I was cast on you;
    from my mother's womb you have been my God.

Do not be far from me,
    for trouble is near
    and there is no one to help.
Many bulls surround me;
    strong bulls of Bashan encircle me.
Roaring lions that tear their prey
    open their mouths wide against me.
I am poured out like water,
    and all my bones are out of joint.
My heart has turned to wax;
    it has melted within me.
My mouth is dried up like a potsherd,
    and my tongue sticks to the roof of my mouth;
    you lay me in the dust of death.
Dogs surround me,
    a pack of villains encircles me;
    they pierce my hands and my feet.
All my bones are on display;
    people stare and gloat over me.
They divide my clothes among them
    and cast lots for my garment.

1. *Have you ever felt forsaken by God? Have you ever felt that God was far from you? That he was not listening to you? What did you do in that situation?*

2. *The Psalmist remembers that God delivered those who trusted him in the past. Does it help to remember this?*

3. *The Psalmist compares his troubles to wild animals—bulls, lions, and dogs. What is the point of this comparison?*

DAY TWO READING AND QUESTIONS

Psalm 22 (NIV)

But you, LORD, do not be far from me.
    You are my strength; come quickly to help me.
Deliver me from the sword,
    my precious life from the power of the dogs.
Rescue me from the mouth of the lions;
    save me from the horns of the wild oxen.
I will declare your name to my people;
    in the assembly I will praise you.
You who fear the LORD, praise him!
    All you descendants of Jacob, honor him!
    Revere him, all you descendants of Israel!
For he has not despised or scorned
    the suffering of the afflicted one;
he has not hidden his face from him
    but has listened to his cry for help.
From you comes the theme of my praise in the great assembly;
    before those who fear you I will fulfill my vows.
The poor will eat and be satisfied;
    those who seek the LORD will praise him—
    may your hearts live forever!
All the ends of the earth
    will remember and turn to the LORD,
and all the families of the nations
    will bow down before him,
for dominion belongs to the LORD
    and he rules over the nations.
All the rich of the earth will feast and worship;
    all who go down to the dust will kneel before him—
    those who cannot keep themselves alive.

Posterity will serve him;
future generations will be told about the LORD.
They will proclaim his righteousness,
declaring to a people yet unborn:
He has done it!

1. *How is the tone of these verses different from that of the previous verses? Why do you think the tone shifts here?*

2. *Who is the focus of these verses?*

3. *Why is there a change from the singular ("My God, my God") in the first half of the Psalm to the plural ("all") in the second half? Why is this significant?*

DAY THREE READING AND QUESTIONS

Psalm 42 (NLT)

As the deer longs for streams of water,
so I long for you, O God.
I thirst for God, the living God.
When can I go and stand before him?
Day and night I have only tears for food,
while my enemies continually taunt me, saying,
"Where is this God of yours?"
My heart is breaking
as I remember how it used to be:
I walked among the crowds of worshipers,
leading a great procession to the house of God,
singing for joy and giving thanks
amid the sound of a great celebration!

Why am I discouraged?
    Why is my heart so sad?
I will put my hope in God!
    I will praise him again—
    my Savior and my God!

1. *How thirsty are we for God? Have you ever longed for God but felt there was no way to find him?*

2. *Have others ever wondered where God was in your life? Have you ever wondered?*

3. *This Psalm touches on the power of memory. Can you recall some times when you especially felt the presence of God? Share those times with others.*

DAY FOUR READING AND QUESTIONS

Psalm 42 (NLT)

Now I am deeply discouraged,
    but I will remember you—
even from distant Mount Hermon, the source of the Jordan,
    from the land of Mount Mizar.
I hear the tumult of the raging seas
    as your waves and surging tides sweep over me.
But each day the LORD pours his unfailing love upon me,
    and through each night I sing his songs,
    praying to God who gives me life.
"O God my rock," I cry,
    "Why have you forgotten me?
Why must I wander around in grief,
    oppressed by my enemies?"

Their taunts break my bones.
    They scoff, "Where is this God of yours?"
Why am I discouraged?
    Why is my heart so sad?
I will put my hope in God!
    I will praise him again—
    my Savior and my God!

1. *Have you ever felt that trouble has overwhelmed you like a flood? ("Your waves and surging tides sweep over me.") Why did you feel that way?*

2. *Can we sincerely sing songs to God through the night when we are flooded with troubles? What allows us to do this?*

3. *How is hope the antidote to feeling downcast?*

DAY FIVE READING AND QUESTIONS

Go back and read Psalms 22 and 42.

1. *Why is Psalm 22 such an appropriate Psalm for Jesus to pray from the cross? Do you think Jesus knew the whole Psalm, including its ending, with trust in God to deliver?*

2. *What things do we "thirst for" besides God? Can those things quench our thirst?*

3. *What moves us from feeling forgotten by God to being sure he is our Savior and God?*

Meditation on Psalms 22 and 42

"Why? Why have you forsaken me? Where are you?" There are times we all have asked this of God.

Should we ask such questions? Doesn't this show a profound lack of faith?

But the Psalmists asked these hard questions. And Jesus asked them. Did they lack faith?

Of course not. But their faith was tested, as ours is tested by circumstances out of our control. It is particularly when we cannot see what God is doing that we are called upon to trust him. And although these laments begin with honest cries of the heart, they end with words of faith and praise.

Thirsty.

We all know what it's like to be thirsty. We may even know what it's like to be thirsty without a drop to drink.

Thirsty for God.

When we sing the words "As the deer pants for water . . ." we usually think of our holy desire for God. But in Psalm 42, the Psalmist thirsts for God but cannot find him. The only drink he finds is his own tears.

And yet he trusts in God. A God who seems to have forgotten him. But still he trusts that God has been, is, and will be his Savior.

What do we do in pain, sickness, poverty, and uncertainty? We cry out *Why*? to God. We might not get an answer to our why. But we will get the answer we really need. God. God alone. The only one who can quench our thirst.

"Water of life, make us thirsty for you. Do not be far from us. May we see your deliverance and proclaim it to new generations."

Consider singing these songs as you continue your meditation: "Blessed Be Your Name" and "As the Deer."

LAMENTS OVER SIN

Psalms 51 and 44

DAY ONE READING AND QUESTIONS

Psalm 51 (NIV)

Have mercy on me, O God,
    according to your unfailing love;
according to your great compassion
    blot out my transgressions.
Wash away all my iniquity
    and cleanse me from my sin.
For I know my transgressions,
    and my sin is always before me.
Against you, you only, have I sinned
    and done what is evil in your sight;
so you are right in your verdict
    and justified when you judge.
Surely I was sinful at birth,
    sinful from the time my mother conceived me.
Yet you desired faithfulness even in the womb;
    you taught me wisdom in that secret place.
Cleanse me with hyssop, and I will be clean;
    wash me, and I will be whiter than snow.
Let me hear joy and gladness;
    let the bones you have crushed rejoice.
Hide your face from my sins
    and blot out all my iniquity.
Create in me a pure heart, O God,
    and renew a steadfast spirit within me.

Do not cast me from your presence
    or take your Holy Spirit from me.
Restore to me the joy of your salvation
    and grant me a willing spirit, to sustain me.

1. *Traditionally this Psalm is associated with David's repentance after his sin with Bathsheba. Read that story in 2 Samuel 11–12. Is Psalm 51 an appropriate response after such a sin? Why or why not?*

2. *David says his sin is against God alone. Yet he sinned against Uriah, Bathsheba, Joab, and others. We also sin against many. How then are our sins against God alone?*

3. *This prayer is for more than forgiveness. It asks for a new heart, a right and Holy Spirit. Why do we need more than forgiveness from God?*

DAY TWO READING AND QUESTIONS

Psalm 51 (NIV)

Then I will teach transgressors your ways,
    so that sinners will turn back to you.
Deliver me from the guilt of bloodshed, O God,
    you who are God my Savior,
    and my tongue will sing of your righteousness.
Open my lips, LORD,
    and my mouth will declare your praise.
You do not delight in sacrifice, or I would bring it;
    you do not take pleasure in burnt offerings.
My sacrifice, O God, is a broken spirit;
    a broken and contrite heart
    you, God, will not despise.
May it please you to prosper Zion,
    to build up the walls of Jerusalem.

Then you will delight in the sacrifices of the righteous,
  in burnt offerings offered whole;
  then bulls will be offered on your altar.

1. *God commanded sacrifices of his people, but this says he has no delight or pleasure in sacrifice. How can both of these be true?*

2. *What is the sacrifice God desires? What does that mean?*

3. *Although this is a deeply personal confession of sin, it ends on the topic of the prosperity of all God's people ("Zion, Jerusalem"). How does personal sin affect all God's people? Is sin ever completely private and individual?*

DAY THREE READING AND QUESTIONS

Psalm 44 (NLT)

O God, we have heard it with our own ears—
  our ancestors have told us
of all you did in their day,
  in days long ago:
You drove out the pagan nations by your power
  and gave all the land to our ancestors.
You crushed their enemies
  and set our ancestors free.
They did not conquer the land with their swords;
  it was not their own strong arm that gave them victory.
It was your right hand and strong arm
  and the blinding light from your face that helped them,
  for you loved them.
You are my King and my God.
  You command victories for Israel.

Only by your power can we push back our enemies;
only in your name can we trample our foes.
I do not trust in my bow;
I do not count on my sword to save me.
You are the one who gives us victory over our enemies;
you disgrace those who hate us.
O God, we give glory to you all day long
and constantly praise your name. *Interlude*
But now you have tossed us aside in dishonor.
You no longer lead our armies to battle.
You make us retreat from our enemies
and allow those who hate us to plunder our land.
You have butchered us like sheep
and scattered us among the nations.
You sold your precious people for a pittance,
making nothing on the sale.
You let our neighbors mock us.
We are an object of scorn and derision to those around us.
You have made us the butt of their jokes;
they shake their heads at us in scorn.
We can't escape the constant humiliation;
shame is written across our faces.
All we hear are the taunts of our mockers.
All we see are our vengeful enemies.

1. *Unlike most laments, this one does not begin with a complaint but with a remembrance of what God has done and praise to him as a delivering king. Would it help us faithfully lament if we began with memory and praise? Why or why not?*

2. *God has tossed his people aside in spite of their praise to him. Why? Have you ever felt abandoned by God when you thought you were trusting in him? Have you ever felt God was treating you unfairly?*

3. *God has allowed others to violently butcher his people and sell them as slaves. He also has allowed others to mock, taunt, and humiliate his people. Which is harder to take: violence or humiliation?*

DAY FOUR READING AND QUESTIONS

Psalm 44 (NLT)

All this has happened though we have not forgotten you.
We have not violated your covenant.
Our hearts have not deserted you.
We have not strayed from your path.
Yet you have crushed us in the jackal's desert home.
You have covered us with darkness and death.
If we had forgotten the name of our God
or spread our hands in prayer to foreign gods,
God would surely have known it,
for he knows the secrets of every heart.
But for your sake we are killed every day;
we are being slaughtered like sheep.
Wake up, O LORD! Why do you sleep?
Get up! Do not reject us forever.
Why do you look the other way?
Why do you ignore our suffering and oppression?
We collapse in the dust,
lying face down in the dirt.
Rise up! Help us!
Ransom us because of your unfailing love.

1. *God knows the secrets of the heart. That means he knows our sins but also knows of our trust. What happens when we trust God and he still allows terrible things to happen to us? What kind of God would do this?*

2. *Do you ever tell God to wake up? To come help? Can we do this with respect for God?*

3. *The Psalm ends with trust in God's unfailing love. How can one think God is (or at least seems) unjust and still trust in his love? What kind of trust is this?*

DAY FIVE READING AND QUESTIONS

Go back and read Psalms 51 and 44.

1. *These Psalms rely on God's unfailing love. Looking at Psalm 51, what might make one doubt God's unfailing love? What might cause that doubt in Psalm 44?*

2. *What is the relationship between sin and faithfulness in these two Psalms? Can one sin and still be faithful to God?*

3. *Do we lament over our sins or do we rush repentance? Can we focus too much on our sins?*

Meditation on Psalms 51 and 44

"I'm sorry."

When I was a kid, these seemed like magic words. "Say you're sorry," Mom would tell me after I terrorized my little brother. So I'd reluctantly say the words and all would be well.

Repentance is more than saying we are sorry. It calls for a radical change of heart and change of life. And our forgiveness is not based on saying the right words, having the right feelings, or even (by themselves) doing the right things. It is based on the mercy and unfailing love of God.

Repentance is more than just "quitting our meanness." It is throwing ourselves on God's mercy. It is complete dependence on him to forgive, to renew our spirit, to cleanse our hearts. Even after repentance, there may be severe consequences of our sins. But we have sinned against God alone, and his mercy restores our relationship with him. This is what our hearts desire—to be right with God, not just to escape from consequences.

But sin isn't the only thing that can separate us from God. Psalm 44 shows that ignorance and doubt also cause us to lament. What happens when we do not understand the God we have? What happens when we do not like the God we have?

When we trust God with all our hearts and still suffer unjustly, we wonder where God is. Why doesn't he do something? When we see little children suffer through no fault of their own, we wonder, "What kind of God would do this to a child?" Or (if you prefer), "What kind of God would allow this to be done to a child?" We might even say, "I cannot believe in that kind of God—a God who would allow that unjust suffering."

But we do not get to choose the God we want. The God revealed in Scripture is the only God we have. But Psalm 44 gives us words to lament our doubt of God. When we do not understand God or even like what he is doing (or not doing), we maintain our trust. Because no matter how it seems, he is the God of unfailing love.

We lament our sins. We lament our inability to understand the ways of God. But we do both in trust.

"God of unfailing love, cleanse our hearts! Show us mercy! Renew your Spirit in us! And increase our trust in you when we cannot understand."

Consider singing these songs as you continue your meditation: "Oh, for a Closer Walk with God" and "Change My Heart, O God."

THANKSGIVING PSALMS

We tend to sing when we are thankful. When we think of Psalms or hymns, we might immediately think of words of gratitude. Again, the Psalms give words to the deepest expressions of our hearts. When we think of what God has done for us in the past, our hearts overflow with thankfulness. When we reflect on how God cares for us each day, we sing of his care. And when we trust God to continue to provide for us tomorrow, we pray these words of gratitude.

THANKSGIVING FOR ANSWERED PRAYERS

Psalms 40 and 116

DAY ONE READING AND QUESTIONS

Psalm 40 (NIV)

I waited patiently for the LORD;
    he turned to me and heard my cry.
He lifted me out of the slimy pit,
    out of the mud and mire;
he set my feet on a rock
    and gave me a firm place to stand.
He put a new song in my mouth,
    a hymn of praise to our God.
Many will see and fear the LORD
    and put their trust in him.
Blessed is the one
    who trusts in the LORD,
who does not look to the proud,
    to those who turn aside to false gods.
Many, LORD my God,
    are the wonders you have done,
    the things you planned for us.
None can compare with you;
    were I to speak and tell of your deeds,
    they would be too many to declare.
Sacrifice and offering you did not desire—
    but my ears you have opened—
    burnt offerings and sin offerings you did not require.
Then I said, "Here I am, I have come—
    it is written about me in the scroll.
I desire to do your will, my God;
    your law is within my heart."

1. *Reflect on the times when God has answered your cry for help. What was your heartfelt reaction in those times?*

2. *How does our thanksgiving to God cause many others to place their trust in him?*

3. *What does it mean to have God's law written in our hearts? Does this give us a different view of the word "law"?*

DAY TWO READING AND QUESTIONS

Psalm 40 (NIV)

I proclaim your saving acts in the great assembly;
    I do not seal my lips, LORD,
    as you know.
I do not hide your righteousness in my heart;
    I speak of your faithfulness and your saving help.
I do not conceal your love and your faithfulness
    from the great assembly.
Do not withhold your mercy from me, LORD;
    may your love and faithfulness always protect me.
For troubles without number surround me;
    my sins have overtaken me, and I cannot see.
They are more than the hairs of my head,
    and my heart fails within me.
Be pleased to save me, LORD;
    come quickly, LORD, to help me.
May all who want to take my life
    be put to shame and confusion;
may all who desire my ruin
    be turned back in disgrace.

May those who say to me, "Aha! Aha!"
be appalled at their own shame.
But may all who seek you
rejoice and be glad in you;
may those who long for your saving help always say,
"The Lord is great!"
But as for me, I am poor and needy;
may the Lord think of me.
You are my help and my deliverer;
you are my God, do not delay.

1. *Why might we be tempted to be quiet and conceal what God has done for us? Why should we speak of his faithfulness and help?*

2. *Even in this thanksgiving Psalm, there is a confession of sin. How is confession related to thanksgiving?*

3. *Why does this thanksgiving Psalm end with a plea for God to not delay his help? Does this show a lack of trust in God?*

DAY THREE READING AND QUESTIONS

Psalm 116 (NLT)

I love the Lord because he hears my voice
and my prayer for mercy.
Because he bends down to listen,
I will pray as long as I have breath!
Death wrapped its ropes around me;
the terrors of the grave overtook me.
I saw only trouble and sorrow.
Then I called on the name of the Lord:
"Please, Lord, save me!"

How kind the LORD is! How good he is!
So merciful, this God of ours!
The LORD protects those of childlike faith;
I was facing death, and he saved me.
Let my soul be at rest again,
for the LORD has been good to me.
He has saved me from death,
my eyes from tears,
my feet from stumbling.
And so I walk in the LORD's presence
as I live here on earth!

1. *Have you ever been close to death? If so (or if you can imagine being close to death), how did you feel when your life was spared?*

2. *Do we love God because he answers our prayers? If so, is there any danger in that motivation for love?*

3. *After God delivers, our souls are at rest. How is rest a gift from God and an answer to our prayers? Do we rest as much as God wants us to?*

DAY FOUR READING AND QUESTIONS

Psalm 116 (NLT)

I believed in you, so I said,
"I am deeply troubled, LORD."
In my anxiety I cried out to you,
"These people are all liars!"
What can I offer the LORD
for all he has done for me?
I will lift up the cup of salvation
and praise the LORD's name for saving me.

I will keep my promises to the LORD
    in the presence of all his people.
The LORD cares deeply
    when his loved ones die.
O LORD, I am your servant;
    yes, I am your servant, born into your household;
    you have freed me from my chains.
I will offer you a sacrifice of thanksgiving
    and call on the name of the LORD.
I will fulfill my vows to the LORD
    in the presence of all his people—
in the house of the LORD
    in the heart of Jerusalem.
Praise the LORD!

1. *"These people are all liars!" Why would the Psalmist say this when he is in distress? What might people be lying about?*

2. *Twice in this Psalm the one who has been delivered from trouble says he will keep his promises or vows. What are vows? Do we make vows to God? Should we? How is this different from bargaining with God?*

3. *The Psalmist has been delivered from death, yet he says the death of God's people is precious to God. Why doesn't God deliver all his precious people from death?*

DAY FIVE READING AND QUESTIONS

Go back and read Psalms 40 and 116.

1. *Psalm 40 begins with "I waited patiently for the LORD to help me." Why do we find it difficult to wait? How can we become more patient?*

2. *Do you find it easier to cry out to God in trouble or to thank him when he answers you? Why? How are these two reactions to God related?*

3. *These Psalms mention telling others about how God has answered our prayers. Are we ever reluctant to do that? Why?*

Meditation on Psalms 40 and 116

Prayer requests. Every church I know has prayer requests in their assembly. These requests are almost always for healing, sometimes with great detail on the person's ailments.

There is nothing wrong with prayer requests. We are to make all our needs known to the Father who loves us.

But, comparatively, far less often do we find thanksgiving for answered prayers in our assemblies. I wonder why that is. Do we take God's healing for granted? Do we think we look proud if we say God answered us? Or do we simply neglect to show gratitude for what God has done?

These Psalms give us examples of publicly thanking God for what he has done. "I have told your people. I have talked about your faithfulness. I have told everyone in the great assembly."

Thanksgiving should be at the center of every assembly of God's people.

What's more, these Psalms say that giving thanks for what God has done is a form of evangelism. "Many will see what he has done and be amazed. They will put their trust in the LORD." We sometimes look for evangelistic methods. Here's one: go and share what God has done for you!

And gratitude is also spiritual formation. "I will fulfill my vows to the LORD." This is more than just an attempt to try harder to live right. It flows from a living relationship of thankfulness to the God who provides. Out of that overflowing gratitude, we keep our promises to love God and to love our neighbors.

Giving thanks is worship, evangelism, and spiritual formation.

"LORD, we love you because you have heard our cries for mercy. You have acted powerfully to save. You have lifted us up so we may walk in your presence. Thank you!"

Consider singing these songs as you continue your meditation: "Now Thank We All Our God" and "Give Thanks."

THANKSGIVING FROM ALL

Psalms 65, 67, and 138

DAY ONE READING AND QUESTIONS

Psalm 65 (NIV)

Praise awaits you, our God, in Zion;
    to you our vows will be fulfilled.
You who answer prayer,
    to you all people will come.
When we were overwhelmed by sins,
    you forgave our transgressions.
Blessed are those you choose
    and bring near to live in your courts!
We are filled with the good things of your house,
    of your holy temple.
You answer us with awesome and righteous deeds,
    God our Savior,
the hope of all the ends of the earth
    and of the farthest seas,
who formed the mountains by your power,
    having armed yourself with strength,
who stilled the roaring of the seas,
    the roaring of their waves,
    and the turmoil of the nations.
The whole earth is filled with awe at your wonders;
    where morning dawns, where evening fades,
    you call forth songs of joy.
You care for the land and water it;
    you enrich it abundantly.

The streams of God are filled with water
  to provide the people with grain,
  for so you have ordained it.
You drench its furrows and level its ridges;
  you soften it with showers and bless its crops.
You crown the year with your bounty,
  and your carts overflow with abundance.
The grasslands of the wilderness overflow;
  the hills are clothed with gladness.
The meadows are covered with flocks
  and the valleys are mantled with grain;
  they shout for joy and sing.

1. *There is praise for answered prayers for individuals, nations, and the created world in this Psalm. How are these three related?*

2. *What is the result of forgiveness of sin in this Psalm? How does that result make us more thankful to God?*

3. *If we have an abundance of food, do we sometimes take for granted that God sends rain for crops and flocks? What can we do to cultivate more gratitude for God's gift of food?*

DAY TWO READING AND QUESTIONS

Psalm 67 (NLT)

May God be merciful and bless us.
  May his face smile with favor on us. *Interlude*
May your ways be known throughout the earth,
  your saving power among people everywhere.
May the nations praise you, O God.
  Yes, may all the nations praise you.

Let the whole world sing for joy,
  because you govern the nations with justice
  and guide the people of the whole world. *Interlude*
May the nations praise you, O God.
  Yes, may all the nations praise you.
Then the earth will yield its harvests,
  and God, our God, will richly bless us.
Yes, God will bless us,
  and people all over the world will fear him.

1. *What does it mean for God's face to smile with favor on us? What do you think of when you think of God's face?*

2. *We usually ask God to bless us because we want or need something. What is the purpose of God's blessing in this Psalm? Does that change how we ask for blessings?*

3. *By faith, we are God's people. Yet this Psalm calls on all people to praise God for his gifts. Do all people belong to God? Even those who do not believe in him?*

DAY THREE READING AND QUESTIONS

Psalm 138 (NIV)

I will praise you, LORD, with all my heart;
  before the "gods" I will sing your praise.
I will bow down toward your holy temple
  and will praise your name
  for your unfailing love and your faithfulness,
for you have so exalted your solemn decree
  that it surpasses your fame.

When I called, you answered me;
  you greatly emboldened me.
May all the kings of the earth praise you, LORD,
  when they hear what you have decreed.
May they sing of the ways of the LORD,
  for the glory of the LORD is great.

1. *What are the "gods" of our age? How do we praise God in front of those "gods"?*

2. *How does God answering our prayers cause the kings of the earth to praise God?*

3. *Who really rules our world: political leaders (like presidents, prime ministers, and kings) or the Lord God? Do we often think of God as ruling all nations? How does he rule them?*

DAY FOUR READING AND QUESTIONS

Psalm 138 (NIV)

Though the LORD is exalted, he looks kindly on the lowly;
  though lofty, he sees them from afar.
Though I walk in the midst of trouble,
  you preserve my life.
You stretch out your hand against the anger of my foes;
  with your right hand you save me.
The LORD will vindicate me;
  your love, LORD, endures forever—
  do not abandon the works of your hands.

1. *How is God beyond us, exalted and lofty? How do we show reverence to that exalted God?*

2. *How are we lowly? What is God's attitude toward the lowly?*

3. *What does it mean to be vindicated? Why do we need vindication? How does God vindicate us?*

DAY FIVE READING AND QUESTIONS

Go back and read Psalms 65, 67, and 138.

1. *These Psalms speak of kings, hills, meadows, and valleys joining in our songs to God. Do we think of the whole world joining in our songs of thanksgiving? If we did, how would this change our experience of worship?*

2. *These Psalms focus on the presence of God in his temple. Where is the temple of God today? How do we experience God's presence in that temple?*

3. *In these Psalms, gratitude turns into praise. What is the relationship between gratitude and praise? What is the difference between them?*

Meditation on Psalms 65, 67, and 138

When God answers our prayer, we give thanks. When he forgives our sins, we give thanks. When he provides for us, we give thanks. When he calls us into his presence, we give thanks.

But we are not alone. We are joined in our songs of gratitude by the whole world. Creation sings its thanks to God. The crops give thanks for the rain. The animals give thanks for food. Even the hills give thanks.

So when we say we are "blessed," let us remember that we are not the only ones who are blessed. The rulers of the nations join us in giving thanks to God. Even those nations that do not worship God or who serve other gods give thanks for rain, sunshine, and food, even though they might not understand the God to whom they pray. All people of the world give thanks to God.

As Jesus reminds us, God "causes his sun to rise on the evil and the good, and sends rain on the righteous and the unrighteous" (Matt. 5:45 NIV). So when we give thanks to our God, the voices of all people, all rulers, and all creation join us in that great song!

"God of love, with all around us we sing of your gracious gifts. Thanks be to God!"

Consider singing these songs as you continue your meditation: "All Creatures of Our God and King" and "All of Creation."

THANKSGIVING FOR STEADFAST LOVE

Psalms 30 and 92

DAY ONE READING AND QUESTIONS

Psalm 30 (NLT)

I will exalt you, Lord, for you rescued me.
    You refused to let my enemies triumph over me.
O Lord my God, I cried to you for help,
    and you restored my health.
You brought me up from the grave, O Lord.
    You kept me from falling into the pit of death.
Sing to the Lord, all you godly ones!
    Praise his holy name.
For his anger lasts only a moment,
    but his favor lasts a lifetime!
Weeping may last through the night,
    but joy comes with the morning.

1. *God saves us from our enemies. God saves us from death. How is death an enemy? How has God saved us from death?*

2. *Is God's anger here associated with sickness and death? If so, if we are sick does that mean God is angry with us? Why or why not?*

3. *Joy comes in the morning. This is encouraging. But why does God allow weeping in the night? Why do we have to wait until morning?*

DAY TWO READING AND QUESTIONS

Psalm 30 (NLT)

When I was prosperous, I said,
  "Nothing can stop me now!"
Your favor, O LORD, made me as secure as a mountain.
  Then you turned away from me, and I was shattered.
I cried out to you, O LORD.
  I begged the LORD for mercy, saying,
"What will you gain if I die,
  if I sink into the grave?
Can my dust praise you?
  Can it tell of your faithfulness?
Hear me, LORD, and have mercy on me.
  Help me, O LORD."
You have turned my mourning into joyful dancing.
  You have taken away my clothes of mourning and clothed
    me with joy,
that I might sing praises to you and not be silent.
  O LORD my God, I will give you thanks forever!

1. *Reflect on times when you felt secure and unshakeable in your faith. Can we feel that way at all times? What can help us have that kind of trust?*

2. *In the Bible, God's people sometimes dance before the Lord. Why? What does that dancing communicate? Do you ever feel like dancing because of God's blessings?*

3. *Even when we are blessed by God, are we sometimes tempted to be silent about it? If so, why?*

DAY THREE READING AND QUESTIONS

Psalm 92 (NIV)

It is good to praise the LORD
and make music to your name, O Most High,
proclaiming your love in the morning
and your faithfulness at night,
to the music of the ten-stringed lyre
and the melody of the harp.
For you make me glad by your deeds, LORD;
I sing for joy at what your hands have done.
How great are your works, LORD,
how profound your thoughts!
Senseless people do not know,
fools do not understand,
that though the wicked spring up like grass
and all evildoers flourish,
they will be destroyed forever.
But you, LORD, are forever exalted.

1. *This Psalm praises God's faithfulness. What does that mean? How has God been faithful to you?*

2. *God's thoughts are profound. His ways are beyond our understanding. Do you sometimes find it difficult to serve a God you cannot understand? What do we do in those times?*

3. *Is understanding God strictly an intellectual exercise? Or does one's heart and moral actions affect that understanding?*

DAY FOUR READING AND QUESTIONS

Psalm 92 (NIV)

For surely your enemies, LORD,
surely your enemies will perish;
all evildoers will be scattered.
You have exalted my horn like that of a wild ox;
fine oils have been poured on me.
My eyes have seen the defeat of my adversaries;
my ears have heard the rout of my wicked foes.
The righteous will flourish like a palm tree,
they will grow like a cedar of Lebanon;
planted in the house of the LORD,
they will flourish in the courts of our God.
They will still bear fruit in old age,
they will stay fresh and green,
proclaiming, "The LORD is upright;
he is my Rock and there is no wickedness in him."

1. *The Psalm speaks of our enemies and God's enemies. Are these always the same? Should they be? How should we treat our enemies? How should we treat God's enemies?*

2. *According to this Psalm, how do God's people stay young, even in old age?*

3. *This Psalm begins and ends with telling of the faithfulness of God. Should we more frequently tell others about the greatness of God?*

DAY FIVE READING AND QUESTIONS

Go back and read Psalms 30 and 92.

1. *Psalm 30 is traditionally associated with the dedication of the temple. Psalm 92 is traditionally a song for the Sabbath. Several countries today celebrate a day of thanksgiving. Is it good to have special occasions focused on giving thanks? Is there a danger in that custom?*

2. *Why do music and singing seem to be the best way to express gratitude?*

3. *God is our rock. What does that mean? How is this an apt picture of God's steadfast love?*

Meditation on Psalms 30 and 92

I think of my dad when I think of rocks. Dad always loved rocks. Walking through the woods, he'd stop, pick up a rock, and admire its beauty. Later, he put rough gemstones in a rock tumbler to bring out their beauty. He made homemade jewelry—rings and pendants—that my wife and mother still wear.

God is our rock. Often the Psalms speak of him that way. But the picture is different from the beautiful rocks my dad collected. Although God is beautiful (he is even beauty itself), the emphasis in the Psalms is that he is unmovable, like a huge outcropping of rock. He is not unmoved by our distress. Instead, he sees and moves powerfully to help us.

But he is a dependable God. In the chaos of our lives, when the ground may shift beneath our feet, he is a firm and unmovable place on which we can stand. He is a Fortress of Rock that provides absolute safety.

So we break out in song to the "Rock of Ages." We hide ourselves in the cleft of the Rock. We go to the Rock who is higher than we are. We stand on the solid Rock. We praise the mighty fortress. We sing of our Rock with joy and gratitude for the shelter, stability, and safety he brings.

"God, our Rock, shelter and protect us. May we stand securely on you alone."

Consider singing these songs as you continue your meditation: "My Hope Is Built on Nothing Less" and "Rock of Ages You Will Stand."

PSALMS OF PRAISE

We sometimes make a distinction between thanksgiving and praise. We give thanks to God because of what he has done for us. We give praise to God because of who God is. Of course, there is much overlap between thanksgiving and praise in the Psalms. If we are thankful to God, we break out in praise. If we praise God, we are also thankful. But it is healthy at times to praise God simply for who he is, not just because he has done something for us. In praise, we stand in awe of the God we serve.

PRAISE FOR CREATION

Psalms 8 and 104

DAY ONE READING AND QUESTIONS

Psalm 8 (NLT)

O LORD, our LORD, your majestic name fills the earth!
    Your glory is higher than the heavens.
You have taught children and infants
    to tell of your strength,
silencing your enemies
    and all who oppose you.
When I look at the night sky and see the work of your fingers—
    the moon and the stars you set in place—
what are mere mortals that you should think about them,
    human beings that you should care for them?
Yet you made them only a little lower than God
    and crowned them with glory and honor.
You gave them charge of everything you made,
    putting all things under their authority—
the flocks and the herds
    and all the wild animals,
the birds in the sky, the fish in the sea,
    and everything that swims the ocean currents.
O LORD, our LORD, your majestic name fills the earth!

1. *What does it mean to say that the Lord's name is majestic? Why is God's name important? What other words come to mind when you hear "majestic"?*

2. *We usually think of children as helpless. How does the praise of children and infants create a stronghold against enemies? How do children and infants praise God?*

3. *God has made humanity the rulers over the rest of creation. What does this rule look like? Are humans to exploit creation for their own purposes? Or do we rule over creation for the sake of the natural world?*

DAY TWO READING AND QUESTIONS

Psalm 104 (NIV)

Praise the LORD, my soul.
LORD my God, you are very great;
  you are clothed with splendor and majesty.
The LORD wraps himself in light as with a garment;
  he stretches out the heavens like a tent
  and lays the beams of his upper chambers on their waters.
He makes the clouds his chariot
  and rides on the wings of the wind.
He makes winds his messengers,
  flames of fire his servants.
He set the earth on its foundations;
  it can never be moved.
You covered it with the watery depths as with a garment;
  the waters stood above the mountains.
But at your rebuke the waters fled,
  at the sound of your thunder they took to flight;
they flowed over the mountains,
  they went down into the valleys,
  to the place you assigned for them.
You set a boundary they cannot cross;
  never again will they cover the earth.

He makes springs pour water into the ravines;
    it flows between the mountains.
They give water to all the beasts of the field;
    the wild donkeys quench their thirst.
The birds of the sky nest by the waters;
    they sing among the branches.
He waters the mountains from his upper chambers;
    the land is satisfied by the fruit of his work.
He makes grass grow for the cattle,
    and plants for people to cultivate—
    bringing forth food from the earth:
wine that gladdens human hearts,
    oil to make their faces shine,
    and bread that sustains their hearts.
The trees of the LORD are well watered,
    the cedars of Lebanon that he planted.
There the birds make their nests;
    the stork has its home in the junipers.
The high mountains belong to the wild goats;
    the crags are a refuge for the hyrax.

1. *God wraps, stretches, makes, gives, sets, covers, and waters in this Psalm. He is a God actively creating the world. Do we sometimes think of God as creating only in the past? How does God act today?*

2. *When we look at the world of nature, do we see it as reflecting God or do we see it merely as a world following natural scientific processes? Is nature a machine, or is God wrapped up in the world?*

3. *God provides wine, oil, and bread for us to make our hearts glad. Do we take the time to truly enjoy our food? Or do we take food for granted? What joy do you get from your meals?*

DAY THREE READING AND QUESTIONS

Psalm 104 (NIV)

He made the moon to mark the seasons,
    and the sun knows when to go down.
You bring darkness, it becomes night,
    and all the beasts of the forest prowl.
The lions roar for their prey
    and seek their food from God.
The sun rises, and they steal away;
    they return and lie down in their dens.
Then people go out to their work,
    to their labor until evening.
How many are your works, LORD!
    In wisdom you made them all;
    the earth is full of your creatures.
There is the sea, vast and spacious,
    teeming with creatures beyond number—
    living things both large and small.
There the ships go to and fro,
    and Leviathan, which you formed to frolic there.

1. *God made time—day, night, and the seasons. Do we live our lives in a healthy rhythm of work and rest? Or have we artificially created our own time and forgotten God's time?*

2. *Think of the variety in God's creation. Why did God make so many types of plants and animals?*

3. *In ancient Hebrew thought, the sea is often considered chaotic. Here God rules over the sea and its creatures. In what other ways does God rule over what seems chaotic to us?*

DAY FOUR READING AND QUESTIONS

Psalm 104 (NIV)

All creatures look to you
to give them their food at the proper time.
When you give it to them,
they gather it up;
when you open your hand,
they are satisfied with good things.
When you hide your face,
they are terrified;
when you take away their breath,
they die and return to the dust.
When you send your Spirit,
they are created,
and you renew the face of the ground.
May the glory of the LORD endure forever;
may the LORD rejoice in his works—
he who looks at the earth, and it trembles,
who touches the mountains, and they smoke.
I will sing to the LORD all my life;
I will sing praise to my God as long as I live.
May my meditation be pleasing to him,
as I rejoice in the LORD.
But may sinners vanish from the earth
and the wicked be no more.
Praise the LORD, my soul.
Praise the LORD.

1. *God not only created the world but he sustains it, giving food to every creature. How often do we think that we rely on God for food? Have you ever been short of food? If we have enough food, is it difficult to truly rely on God for our daily bread?*

2. *Death is also in the hands of God. Is death a part of creation? Does God send death? If so, how can he be a good God?*

3. *Song and meditation are connected in this Psalm. As you meditate on the Psalms, do songs come to mind? Why does it seem natural to sing Psalms?*

DAY FIVE READING AND QUESTIONS

Go back and read Psalms 8 and 104.

1. *Psalm 8 celebrates the honored role God has given to humans. Do we sometimes think too little of what humanity can do? Do we sometimes think too much of ourselves as humans? What would be a true measure of our human worth?*

2. *Do we sometimes make too much of nature, almost worshipping her? Do we sometimes think too little of nature? What is a true measure of the worth of the natural world?*

3. *Although these Psalms say a lot about creation, their focus is on the God who made and who wraps himself with creation. How does praise for what we see always turn us back to the God we cannot see?*

Meditation on Psalms 8 and 104

It is early spring. The trees and bushes have begun to bloom with bright whites, reds, pinks, and yellows. Flowers will follow soon with a wide palette of color. What seemed dead a few days ago now bursts with vibrant life.

From my back porch, I watch birds of every shape and color. One patiently makes a nest near me. Less often, I see deer, foxes, groundhogs, frogs, turtles, and bees.

The sky is blue with wispy clouds that glide over the hills.

All this from my back porch. Not to mention the amazing places the rest of the world has to offer—lakes, canyons, mountains, volcanoes—as well as plants and animals of every kind. Our eyes cannot get enough of the varied beauty that surrounds us.

That beauty forms a lump in one's throat and an expansion of one's chest that can only be expressed by an overused word: "Awesome!" Or, in the words of these Psalms, "majesty," "splendor," "greatness," and "glory."

Here it is important to distinguish: that lump in our throat and expansion of our chest is not caused by the splendor of nature but by meditating on the God who called it all into being—the God who clothes himself in its beauty, the God who sustains it all by his loving hand. He is the God who formed his greatest creature—humanity—from the dust of the ground and who breathed the Spirit of life into this apex of creation.

Who are we? Not much, it would seem, when we look at the awesomeness around us. But who are we? Those crowned with glory and honor by God.

"Creator God, open our eyes to see you in everything around us. And open our eyes to our own beauty, the beauty of being loved by you."

Consider singing these songs as you continue your meditation: "For the Beauty of the Earth" and "How Majestic Is Your Name."

PRAISE FOR WORKS

Psalms 111 and 145

DAY ONE READING AND QUESTIONS

Psalm 111 (NLT)

Praise the LORD!
I will thank the LORD with all my heart
as I meet with his godly people.
How amazing are the deeds of the LORD!
All who delight in him should ponder them.
Everything he does reveals his glory and majesty.
His righteousness never fails.
He causes us to remember his wonderful works.
How gracious and merciful is our LORD!
He gives food to those who fear him;
he always remembers his covenant.

1. *What is the value of praising God with others?*

2. *What works of God are mentioned in this Psalm? Are these in addition to creation? What comes to mind when you think of God working?*

3. *What does it mean that God remembers his covenant? Can God forget anything?*

DAY TWO READING AND QUESTIONS

Psalm 111 (NLT)

He has shown his great power to his people
 by giving them the lands of other nations.
All he does is just and good,
 and all his commandments are trustworthy.
They are forever true,
 to be obeyed faithfully and with integrity.
He has paid a full ransom for his people.
 He has guaranteed his covenant with them forever.
 What a holy, awe-inspiring name he has!
Fear of the LORD is the foundation of true wisdom.
 All who obey his commandments will grow in wisdom.
Praise him forever!

1. *What does it mean that God's works are just, good, trustworthy, and true?*

2. *What does "ransom" mean? How is it related to God's covenant?*

3. *What is fear of the LORD? How is it different from being afraid of God?*

DAY THREE READING AND QUESTIONS

Psalm 145 (NIV)

I will exalt you, my God the King;
 I will praise your name for ever and ever.
Every day I will praise you
 and extol your name for ever and ever.
Great is the LORD and most worthy of praise;
 his greatness no one can fathom.

One generation commends your works to another;
 they tell of your mighty acts.
They speak of the glorious splendor of your majesty—
 and I will meditate on your wonderful works.
They tell of the power of your awesome works—
 and I will proclaim your great deeds.
They celebrate your abundant goodness
 and joyfully sing of your righteousness.
The LORD is gracious and compassionate,
 slow to anger and rich in love.

1. *We cannot fathom the greatness of God. Does it help to try to imagine God? What helps you think about who God is?*

2. *Do we tell of God's works to a new generation? How can we best do this?*

3. *What does it mean that God is slow to anger? How does that relate to his steadfast love?*

DAY FOUR READING AND QUESTIONS

Psalm 145 (NIV)

The LORD is good to all;
 he has compassion on all he has made.
All your works praise you, LORD;
 your faithful people extol you.
They tell of the glory of your kingdom
 and speak of your might,
so that all people may know of your mighty acts
 and the glorious splendor of your kingdom.

Your kingdom is an everlasting kingdom,
    and your dominion endures through all generations.
The LORD is trustworthy in all he promises
    and faithful in all he does.
The LORD upholds all who fall
    and lifts up all who are bowed down.
The eyes of all look to you,
    and you give them their food at the proper time.
You open your hand
    and satisfy the desires of every living thing.
The LORD is righteous in all his ways
    and faithful in all he does.
The LORD is near to all who call on him,
    to all who call on him in truth.
He fulfills the desires of those who fear him;
    he hears their cry and saves them.
The LORD watches over all who love him,
    but all the wicked he will destroy.
My mouth will speak in praise of the LORD.
    Let every creature praise his holy name
    for ever and ever.

1. *Name some ways in which God is good to all people.*

2. *Why is it encouraging that the Lord's kingdom is everlasting? Does any human kingdom or nation last? Why do we act as if they will?*

3. *Does God fulfill all our desires?*

DAY FIVE READING AND QUESTIONS

Go back and read Psalms 111 and 145.

1. *In Hebrew, Psalms 111 and 145 are acrostics—that is, each line begins with a different Hebrew letter in the order of their alphabet. How do these Psalms praise God completely—from "a" to "z"? Can we completely praise our God?*

2. *Psalm 145 praises God as king. Have you ever lived in a country ruled by a king? How do you feel about kings? What does it look like to serve God as our king?*

3. *God's kingship is for all time and for all people. Do we ever limit God's rule and favor to our nation, church, or group? Should we?*

Meditation on Psalms 111 and 145

God is at work. We may think of God's work as creating the world and then resting on the seventh day. But whatever God's rest may mean, it does not mean inaction. The Psalms celebrate the continuing work of God.

He works to feed. We rely on him for daily bread.

He works to give his people land and nations. Every nation on earth exists because of God's powerful work.

He works to give his precepts, his loving instruction, to his people. And that instruction is trustworthy.

He works to redeem his people, to set them free from the slavery of self and of sin.

He works to rule the world. His kingdom has no boundaries and has no end.

And how do we describe these works of God? Great, glorious, and majestic. Righteous, gracious, and compassionate. Trustworthy, faithful, and enduring.

Like the Psalmist, each day we keep these truths before us: God is at work among us. God is at work within us. We praise him for his astounding works!

"Powerful God, open our eyes to what you are doing in your world. You are our king! Rule in our lives today."

Consider singing these songs as you continue your meditation: "God Moves in a Mysterious Way" and "Magnificat."

PRAISE FOR LAW AND LOVE

Psalms 19 and 103

DAY ONE READING AND QUESTIONS

Psalm 19 (NLT)

The heavens proclaim the glory of God.
    The skies display his craftsmanship.
Day after day they continue to speak;
    night after night they make him known.
They speak without a sound or word;
    their voice is never heard.
Yet their message has gone throughout the earth,
    and their words to all the world.
God has made a home in the heavens for the sun.
It bursts forth like a radiant bridegroom after his wedding.
    It rejoices like a great athlete eager to run the race.
The sun rises at one end of the heavens
    and follows its course to the other end.
    Nothing can hide from its heat.
The instructions of the LORD are perfect,
    reviving the soul.
The decrees of the LORD are trustworthy,
    making wise the simple.
The commandments of the LORD are right,
    bringing joy to the heart.
The commands of the LORD are clear,
    giving insight for living.
Reverence for the LORD is pure,
    lasting forever.
The laws of the LORD are true;
    each one is fair.

1. *How do the heavens speak without language? What do the heavens say?*

2. *This Psalm moves abruptly from the heavens praising God to words praising the law. Why does this switch of topics seem awkward to us?*

3. *The law of the Lord is connected here with the fear of the Lord. How are they related?*

DAY TWO READING AND QUESTIONS

Psalm 19 (NLT)

They are more desirable than gold,
    even the finest gold.
They are sweeter than honey,
    even honey dripping from the comb.
They are a warning to your servant,
    a great reward for those who obey them.
How can I know all the sins lurking in my heart?
    Cleanse me from these hidden faults.
Keep your servant from deliberate sins!
    Don't let them control me.
Then I will be free of guilt
    and innocent of great sin.
May the words of my mouth
    and the meditation of my heart
be pleasing to you,
    O LORD, my rock and my redeemer.

1. *What is your reaction to the word "law"? Do you immediately think of the law as precious like gold or sweet like honey?*

2. *This Psalmist asks for forgiveness from hidden faults. How do we hide our faults from ourselves?*

3. *What is the relationship between our words and our heart?*

DAY THREE READING AND QUESTIONS

Psalm 103 (NIV)

Praise the LORD, my soul;
    all my inmost being, praise his holy name.
Praise the LORD, my soul,
    and forget not all his benefits—
who forgives all your sins
    and heals all your diseases,
who redeems your life from the pit
    and crowns you with love and compassion,
who satisfies your desires with good things
    so that your youth is renewed like the eagle's.
The LORD works righteousness
    and justice for all the oppressed.
He made known his ways to Moses,
    his deeds to the people of Israel:
The LORD is compassionate and gracious,
    slow to anger, abounding in love.
He will not always accuse,
    nor will he harbor his anger forever;
he does not treat us as our sins deserve
    or repay us according to our iniquities.
For as high as the heavens are above the earth,
    so great is his love for those who fear him;
as far as the east is from the west,
    so far has he removed our transgressions from us.

1. *We praise God from the soul, our inmost being. What is the soul? How does it praise God?*

2. *God is praised for healing and provision, but also for bringing righteousness and justice. How do we join with God to bring justice to all the oppressed? What does this justice look like in your own community?*

3. *God's grace is linked here with revealing his will to Moses. How is God's love revealed in his words to his people?*

DAY FOUR READING AND QUESTIONS

Psalm 103 (NIV)

As a father has compassion on his children,
    so the LORD has compassion on those who fear him;
for he knows how we are formed,
    he remembers that we are dust.
The life of mortals is like grass,
    they flourish like a flower of the field;
the wind blows over it and it is gone,
    and its place remembers it no more.
But from everlasting to everlasting
    the LORD's love is with those who fear him,
    and his righteousness with their children's children—
with those who keep his covenant
    and remember to obey his precepts.
The LORD has established his throne in heaven,
    and his kingdom rules over all.
Praise the LORD, you his angels,
    you mighty ones who do his bidding,
    who obey his word.

Praise the LORD, all his heavenly hosts,
    you his servants who do his will.
Praise the LORD, all his works
    everywhere in his dominion.
Praise the LORD, my soul.

1. *How does realizing that we are as fragile as grass or dust make us appreciate God's compassion?*

2. *How is God's love connected with keeping his covenant and obeying his precepts? Does obedience earn God's love?*

3. *How is our praise like that of the angels and the heavenly army? How is it different?*

DAY FIVE READING AND QUESTIONS

Go back and read Psalms 19 and 103.

1. *Law. Statutes. Precepts. Commands. Do we often connect these words with the word "love"? Why not?*

2. *Does the description of "law" here contradict the teaching of the apostle Paul that we are not saved by keeping the law?*

3. *What is the purpose of the law in these Psalms?*

Meditation on Psalms 19 and 103

The word "law" does not warm my heart. When I think of law, I think of arbitrary rules and bureaucratic statutes. We even laugh at outdated laws against, say, spitting on the sidewalk that are unrelated to contemporary life. When I think of law, I see authoritarian fathers and officials who "lay down the law" and expect everyone to follow the fine print and the letter of the law.

But the Psalmist praises God for his law. He gives thanks for precepts and statutes. He treasures the law like gold. He craves it like honey.

Can we feel this way about the law? Should we? "Law" is an unfortunate translation of the Hebrew word "Torah." A better translation would be "instruction." In the Bible, we have not a list of arbitrary laws but God's fatherly instruction to his people, inviting them to live in covenant with him. He is not the stern father who lays down the law but a loving parent who teaches his children the best way to live.

When I was a kid, there was something Dad wanted me to do—I can't remember what—and I didn't want to do it. I said, "But Dad, I'm a good kid who always does what you say." He answered, "You do what I say most of the time because you want to do it. Obedience happens only when you don't want to do what I say but you do it anyway."

It's the same way with our God. There are times when we do not understand or even like his commands. But if we know God loves us, we obey out of love.

Love and law. They are inseparable in these Psalms. Love and obedience. They also go together. We do not earn God's love through obedience. His gracious love is free to all. But when we know and trust that love, it makes us more willing to obey.

"God of love, may we love the ways you teach us—your laws, statutes, precepts, and commands."

Consider singing these songs as you continue your meditation: "Ancient Words" and "O How Love I Thy Law."

MEDITATIONS

PART TWO

PRAYING PSALMS OF AFFIRMATION AND CELEBRATION

SPECIAL OCCASION PSALMS

There are songs we sing on special occasions—birthdays, patriotic holidays, and religious holidays. It's the same way with the Psalms. At times, Israel would gather to reaffirm their loyalty to God's covenant. There are Psalms for that. At other times, they would gather to anoint a new king. Since God is the ultimate king of his people, the Psalms for those occasions were what we would call both political and religious. Sometimes Israel would break out in song to praise their earthly king and to praise God, their heavenly king. And they also would sing as they traveled to the great feasts—Passover, Pentecost, and Tabernacles—singing songs of Zion, the city of the great king.

Although we might not celebrate these exact occasions, these Psalms can give us words to sing as we celebrate God's loyalty to and reign over his covenant people.

COVENANT RENEWAL

Psalms 50 and 81

DAY ONE READING AND QUESTIONS

Psalm 50 (NLT)

The LORD, the Mighty One, is God,
    and he has spoken;
he has summoned all humanity
    from where the sun rises to where it sets.
From Mount Zion, the perfection of beauty,
    God shines in glorious radiance.
Our God approaches,
    and he is not silent.
Fire devours everything in his way,
    and a great storm rages around him.
He calls on the heavens above and earth below
    to witness the judgment of his people.
"Bring my faithful people to me—
    those who made a covenant with me by giving sacrifices."
Then let the heavens proclaim his justice,
    for God himself will be the judge. *Interlude*
"O my people, listen as I speak.
    Here are my charges against you, O Israel:
    I am God, your God!
I have no complaint about your sacrifices
    or the burnt offerings you constantly offer.
But I do not need the bulls from your barns
    or the goats from your pens.
For all the animals of the forest are mine,
    and I own the cattle on a thousand hills.

I know every bird on the mountains,
    and all the animals of the field are mine.
If I were hungry, I would not tell you,
    for all the world is mine and everything in it.
Do I eat the meat of bulls?
    Do I drink the blood of goats?
Make thankfulness your sacrifice to God,
    and keep the vows you made to the Most High.
Then call on me when you are in trouble,
    and I will rescue you,
    and you will give me glory."

1. *Do we often think of God as both powerful and beautiful? How do these ideas go together?*

2. *God addresses those who have made a covenant with him. What is a covenant? How does God make a covenant with his people? How do his people renew and keep the covenant?*

3. *Does God need our sacrifices? Then why does he ask for them?*

DAY TWO READING AND QUESTIONS

Psalm 50 (NLT)

But God says to the wicked:
"Why bother reciting my decrees
    and pretending to obey my covenant?
For you refuse my discipline
    and treat my words like trash.
When you see thieves, you approve of them,
    and you spend your time with adulterers.

Your mouth is filled with wickedness,
    and your tongue is full of lies.
You sit around and slander your brother—
    your own mother's son.
While you did all this, I remained silent,
    and you thought I didn't care.
But now I will rebuke you,
    listing all my charges against you.
Repent, all of you who forget me,
    or I will tear you apart,
    and no one will help you.
But giving thanks is a sacrifice that truly honors me.
    If you keep to my path,
    I will reveal to you the salvation of God."

1. *Can one remain in covenant with God and join with thieves and adulterers? Why would one do so and still claim to be in covenant with God?*

2. *How does the way the wicked speak show that they do not keep the covenant?*

3. *When God keeps silent and does not immediately punish us, do we begin to think he is evil like we are? Do God's people sometimes cause others to think less of God?*

DAY THREE READING AND QUESTIONS

Psalm 81 (NIV)

Sing for joy to God our strength;
    shout aloud to the God of Jacob!
Begin the music, strike the timbrel,
    play the melodious harp and lyre.

Sound the ram's horn at the New Moon,
    and when the moon is full, on the day of our festival;
this is a decree for Israel,
    an ordinance of the God of Jacob.
When God went out against Egypt,
    he established it as a statute for Joseph.
I heard an unknown voice say:
"I removed the burden from their shoulders;
    their hands were set free from the basket.
In your distress you called and I rescued you,
    I answered you out of a thundercloud;
    I tested you at the waters of Meribah.
Hear me, my people, and I will warn you—
    if you would only listen to me, Israel!
You shall have no foreign god among you;
    you shall not worship any god other than me.
I am the LORD your God,
    who brought you up out of Egypt.
Open wide your mouth and I will fill it."

1. *This Psalm celebrates the new moon festival with joyous song. What are some holidays we celebrate with songs? How are our celebrations similar to or different from this one?*

2. *What story of Israel is pictured in these verses? Why would that story call forth celebration?*

3. *According to this Psalm, what keeps God from blessing his people?*

DAY FOUR READING AND QUESTIONS

Psalm 81 (NIV)

"But my people would not listen to me;
    Israel would not submit to me.
So I gave them over to their stubborn hearts
    to follow their own devices.
If my people would only listen to me,
    if Israel would only follow my ways,
how quickly I would subdue their enemies
    and turn my hand against their foes!
Those who hate the LORD would cringe before him,
    and their punishment would last forever.
But you would be fed with the finest of wheat;
    with honey from the rock I would satisfy you."

1. *What does it mean to listen to God? How do we show we are listening?*

2. *Is it a good thing when God lets us do what we want? Why or why not?*

3. *How did God feed Israel in the wilderness? How does he feed us today?*

DAY FIVE READING AND QUESTIONS

Go back and read Psalms 50 and 81.

1. *How can we renew our covenant with the Lord today? What rituals or ceremonies might we use?*

2. *The covenant is based on what God has done for his people. What has God done for you?*

3. *These Psalms call on God's people to listen to him. How can we practice listening to God?*

Meditation on Psalms 50 and 81

It's a party!

And at every good party, there's music. At a birthday party, you know the song you will sing. At other parties, there's a band or a DJ.

This is a party to joyously praise our God, the Lord who has made a covenant with us. God shows up at our party, the ultimate "A list" celebrity. And look at how he is dressed, wrapped in beauty and flashing fire!

Since God shows up, this party is also a solemn celebration. It is a time when we reaffirm our commitment to God's covenant. Perhaps you or others you know have reaffirmed your marriage vows in a joyful but solemn ceremony, followed by a party. That is the picture here. We made our vows to God in baptism, and he vowed to be our God and provide for us. He has kept his covenant. So should we.

But the genuine test of reaffirmed marriage vows is how we treat our spouse each day. We must listen to them. The same is true with our covenant with God. It does no good to claim to follow God if we do not listen to him. We listen to him in Scripture. We listen to him in creation. We listen to him in all the events of life. And listening means we obey.

And yes, obedience can be a party!

"Faithful God, we celebrate your dependable grace. Open our hearts and lives to listen, to obey, and to rejoice."

Consider singing these songs as you continue your meditation: "Great Is Thy Faithfulness" and "Shout Hallelujah."

ROYAL PSALMS

Psalms 72 and 2

DAY ONE READING AND QUESTIONS

Psalm 72 (NLT)

Give your love of justice to the king, O God,
  and righteousness to the king's son.
Help him judge your people in the right way;
  let the poor always be treated fairly.
May the mountains yield prosperity for all,
  and may the hills be fruitful.
Help him to defend the poor,
  to rescue the children of the needy,
  and to crush their oppressors.
May they fear you as long as the sun shines,
  as long as the moon remains in the sky.
  Yes, forever!
May the king's rule be refreshing like spring rain on freshly cut grass,
  like the showers that water the earth.
May all the godly flourish during his reign.
  May there be abundant prosperity until the moon is no more.
May he reign from sea to sea,
  and from the Euphrates River to the ends of the earth.
Desert nomads will bow before him;
  his enemies will fall before him in the dust.
The western kings of Tarshish and other distant lands
  will bring him tribute.
The eastern kings of Sheba and Seba
  will bring him gifts.
All kings will bow before him,
  and all nations will serve him.

1. *Traditionally this Psalm is a prayer of David for Solomon. Should we pray for our political leaders ("kings")? How can this Psalm be a model for those prayers?*

2. *This Psalm recognizes that God is the true king who brings justice for his people. What can we do to remind ourselves that God is our true king, not our political leaders?*

3. *Is it right for us to pray that our nation might prosper? When can prayers for prosperity be wrong?*

DAY TWO READING AND QUESTIONS

Psalm 72 (NLT)

He will rescue the poor when they cry to him;
  he will help the oppressed, who have no one to defend them.
He feels pity for the weak and the needy,
  and he will rescue them.
He will redeem them from oppression and violence,
  for their lives are precious to him.
Long live the king!
  May the gold of Sheba be given to him.
May the people always pray for him
  and bless him all day long.
May there be abundant grain throughout the land,
  flourishing even on the hilltops.
May the fruit trees flourish like the trees of Lebanon,
  and may the people thrive like grass in a field.
May the king's name endure forever;
  may it continue as long as the sun shines.
May all nations be blessed through him
  and bring him praise.

Praise the Lord God, the God of Israel,
who alone does such wonderful things.
Praise his glorious name forever!
Let the whole earth be filled with his glory.
Amen and amen!
(This ends the prayers of David son of Jesse.)

1. *How are all nations to be blessed through the king of Israel?*

2. *The king should defend and deliver the afflicted and the needy. How can we ensure that the leaders of today do the same?*

3. *Why does this Psalm, centered on Israel's king, end with praise to the Lord?*

DAY THREE READING AND QUESTIONS

Psalm 2 (NIV)

Why do the nations conspire
and the peoples plot in vain?
The kings of the earth rise up
and the rulers band together
against the Lord and against his anointed, saying,
"Let us break their chains
and throw off their shackles."
The One enthroned in heaven laughs;
the Lord scoffs at them.
He rebukes them in his anger
and terrifies them in his wrath, saying,
"I have installed my king
on Zion, my holy mountain."

1. *The nations conspire against the Lord and his anointed—that is, the king of Israel. Do nations conspire against the Lord today? Does God have an anointed nation today?*

2. *Why does God laugh here? What kind of laughter is this?*

3. *What is the wrath of God? Should we be terrified by his wrath?*

DAY FOUR READING AND QUESTIONS

Psalm 2 (NIV)

I will proclaim the LORD's decree:
He said to me, "You are my son;
    today I have become your father.
Ask me,
    and I will make the nations your inheritance,
    the ends of the earth your possession.
You will break them with a rod of iron;
    you will dash them to pieces like pottery."
Therefore, you kings, be wise;
    be warned, you rulers of the earth.
Serve the LORD with fear
    and celebrate his rule with trembling.
Kiss his son, or he will be angry
    and your way will lead to your destruction,
for his wrath can flare up in a moment.
    Blessed are all who take refuge in him.

1. *Who is the son in these verses? How is he the son of God?*

2. *This king reigns from Zion, a small hill in Jerusalem. Yet God promises this king he will reign over all the earth. What does this mean? How can this be?*

3. *How do the kings of the earth serve the Lord with fear and trembling? Do we serve him in this way?*

DAY FIVE READING AND QUESTIONS

Go back and read Psalms 72 and 2.

1. *Psalm 72 speaks of the king ruling not through military might but by protecting the poor. Is this unrealistic? Could a political leader rule a country this way today?*

2. *Are these merely patriotic Psalms? Or do they look beyond any one nation as the people of God?*

3. *Psalm 2 is understood by Christians as a messianic Psalm, pointing to Jesus. What words in the Psalm lead to that interpretation? Is the Psalm about the kings of ancient Israel or about Jesus?*

Meditation on Psalms 72 and 2

"God save the queen!"

"God bless America!"

We shout and sing these words when we are feeling patriotic. Citizens love their nation, no matter what nation it is, and ask God to bless it. There's nothing wrong with that.

But if we are not careful, those prayers become harmful. We can easily think not just that our nation is the best but that other nations are vastly inferior. We can ask God to bless our nation instead of others—or even at the expense of others. We slip easily from patriotism to nationalism to jingoism. We are the most righteous nation, so God bless us, not them. God is on our side, right or wrong.

The Psalms rightly praise and pray for the king of Israel. But God always intended Israel to be a light to the nations, a blessing to the whole world. God's people sometimes forgot that and rejoiced in being chosen while others were not.

These two Psalms remind the king that God alone rules. God gives justice through the king. God cares for the poor and oppressed through the king. God calls the king his son. But this does not mean the king has all authority by divine right. "Son" here is not a status but a calling. If the king is truly a son, then he will rule like his Father. He will show the compassion and justice of God.

So let us pray for our rulers. But we must not confuse them with the one who is Lord of all.

"King of all creation, rule your people throughout the world. Bless every nation, no exceptions."

Consider singing these songs as you continue your meditation: "O Worship the King" and "Sing to the King."

ENTHRONEMENT PSALMS

Psalms 24, 29, 95, and 97

DAY ONE READING AND QUESTIONS

Psalm 24 (NLT)

The earth is the LORD's, and everything in it.
The world and all its people belong to him.
For he laid the earth's foundation on the seas
and built it on the ocean depths.
Who may climb the mountain of the LORD?
Who may stand in his holy place?
Only those whose hands and hearts are pure,
who do not worship idols
and never tell lies.
They will receive the LORD's blessing
and have a right relationship with God their savior.
Such people may seek you
and worship in your presence, O God of Jacob. *Interlude*
Open up, ancient gates!
Open up, ancient doors,
and let the King of glory enter.
Who is the King of glory?
The LORD, strong and mighty;
the LORD, invincible in battle.
Open up, ancient gates!
Open up, ancient doors,
and let the King of glory enter.
Who is the King of glory?
The LORD of Heaven's Armies—
he is the King of glory. *Interlude*

1. *What gives the Lord God the right to rule over all the earth?*

2. *What does it mean to have clean hands and a pure heart? How do these make one worthy to stand in the presence of God?*

3. *What does "glory" mean? Why is God called the King of Glory?*

DAY TWO READING AND QUESTIONS

Psalm 29 (NIV)

Ascribe to the LORD, you heavenly beings,
ascribe to the LORD glory and strength.
Ascribe to the LORD the glory due his name;
worship the LORD in the splendor of his holiness.
The voice of the LORD is over the waters;
the God of glory thunders,
the LORD thunders over the mighty waters.
The voice of the LORD is powerful;
the voice of the LORD is majestic.
The voice of the LORD breaks the cedars;
the LORD breaks in pieces the cedars of Lebanon.
He makes Lebanon leap like a calf,
Sirion like a young wild ox.
The voice of the LORD strikes
with flashes of lightning.
The voice of the LORD shakes the desert;
the LORD shakes the Desert of Kadesh.
The voice of the LORD twists the oaks
and strips the forests bare.
And in his temple all cry, "Glory!"
The LORD sits enthroned over the flood;
the LORD is enthroned as King forever.

The LORD gives strength to his people;
the LORD blesses his people with peace.

1. *What is holiness? How does holiness relate to God as our King?*

2. *What comes to mind when you think of the "voice of the LORD"? How does God speak in this Psalm?*

3. *Does the Lord demand worship? Why?*

DAY THREE READING AND QUESTIONS

Psalm 95 (NLT)

Come, let us sing to the LORD!
Let us shout joyfully to the Rock of our salvation.
Let us come to him with thanksgiving.
Let us sing psalms of praise to him.
For the LORD is a great God,
a great King above all gods.
He holds in his hands the depths of the earth
and the mightiest mountains.
The sea belongs to him, for he made it.
His hands formed the dry land, too.
Come, let us worship and bow down.
Let us kneel before the LORD our maker,
for he is our God.
We are the people he watches over,
the flock under his care.
If only you would listen to his voice today!
The LORD says, "Don't harden your hearts as Israel did at Meribah,
as they did at Massah in the wilderness.

For there your ancestors tested and tried my patience,
 even though they saw everything I did.
For forty years I was angry with them, and I said,
'They are a people whose hearts turn away from me.
 They refuse to do what I tell them.'
So in my anger I took an oath:
 'They will never enter my place of rest.'"

1. *This Psalm calls for bowing and kneeling before the Lord as our king. Do you regularly bow and kneel before God? Should you? How do we pray and praise God with our bodies?*

2. *Read the stories of Meribah and Massah in Exodus 17:1–7. Why does Psalm 95 turn from praising God in song to a strong warning?*

3. *This Psalm speaks of entering God's rest. What is this rest? How does resting relate to God as our king?*

DAY FOUR READING AND QUESTIONS

Psalm 97 (NIV)

The LORD reigns, let the earth be glad;
 let the distant shores rejoice.
Clouds and thick darkness surround him;
 righteousness and justice are the foundation of his throne.
Fire goes before him
 and consumes his foes on every side.
His lightning lights up the world;
 the earth sees and trembles.
The mountains melt like wax before the LORD,
 before the LORD of all the earth.

The heavens proclaim his righteousness,
　　and all peoples see his glory.
All who worship images are put to shame,
　　those who boast in idols—
　　worship him, all you gods!
Zion hears and rejoices
　　and the villages of Judah are glad
　　because of your judgments, LORD.
For you, LORD, are the Most High over all the earth;
　　you are exalted far above all gods.
Let those who love the LORD hate evil,
　　for he guards the lives of his faithful ones
　　and delivers them from the hand of the wicked.
Light shines on the righteous
　　and joy on the upright in heart.
Rejoice in the LORD, you who are righteous,
　　and praise his holy name.

1. *Do we often think of God as consuming fire? How does this picture of God square with the Lord's righteousness and justice?*

2. *Idol worshippers are put to shame, yet the gods worship the Lord. Are there other gods besides the Lord? In what sense do they worship him?*

3. *What does it mean to hate evil? Does this mean we hate evil people?*

DAY FIVE READING AND QUESTIONS

Go back and read Psalms 24, 29, 95, and 97.

1. *God the King calls us his flock. How does being sheep with a shepherd change our view of God as King?*

2. *How does the idea of God as Creator relate to God as King?*

3. *What blessings does the Lord give to his people as our King?*

Meditation on Psalms 24, 29, 95, and 97

Given the historic track record of kings, democracy sounds like a good idea. But let's not fool ourselves. As God's people, we have a King—an absolute ruler who demands absolute obedience.

But he is not a tyrant. He is a benevolent monarch who rules for our own good.

According to these Psalms, what does God do for us, his subjects?

He creates. By his powerful word, he sustains creation. All that exists in its power and beauty comes from his hand.

What's more, our King fights for us. This has always been the role of kings. Our King fights against all who threaten us. He conquers all his foes and our foes. He thunders against them from on high.

But he is more than a conquering king. He is a gentle shepherd. We are his flock, his helpless sheep. And he generously feeds, protects, and comforts us.

In short, our King blesses us beyond what we deserve, beyond what we can imagine.

And so we joyfully praise him! We wholeheartedly obey him. We exalt him above all.

"Our LORD and King, rule our lives by your grace this day! We shout and sing with our whole being to you, King over all."

Consider singing these songs as you continue your meditation: "Come, Now Is the Time to Worship" and "To God Be the Glory."

SONGS OF ZION AND JERUSALEM

Psalms 48, 84, and 122

DAY ONE READING AND QUESTIONS

Psalm 48 (NLT)

How great is the Lord,
  how deserving of praise,
in the city of our God,
  which sits on his holy mountain!
It is high and magnificent;
  the whole earth rejoices to see it!
Mount Zion, the holy mountain,
  is the city of the great King!
God himself is in Jerusalem's towers,
  revealing himself as its defender.
The kings of the earth joined forces
  and advanced against the city.
But when they saw it, they were stunned;
  they were terrified and ran away.
They were gripped with terror
  and writhed in pain like a woman in labor.
You destroyed them like the mighty ships of Tarshish
  shattered by a powerful east wind.
We had heard of the city's glory,
  but now we have seen it ourselves—
  the city of the Lord of Heaven's Armies.
It is the city of our God;
  he will make it safe forever. *Interlude*

1. *Where is Zion? Why is Zion important?*

2. *Isn't God everywhere? How can one city be his when all the earth is his?*

3. *What does God do for the city of Zion?*

DAY TWO READING AND QUESTIONS

Psalm 48 (NLT)

O God, we meditate on your unfailing love
    as we worship in your Temple.
As your name deserves, O God,
    you will be praised to the ends of the earth.
    Your strong right hand is filled with victory.
Let the people on Mount Zion rejoice.
    Let all the towns of Judah be glad
    because of your justice.
Go, inspect the city of Jerusalem.
    Walk around and count the many towers.
Take note of the fortified walls,
    and tour all the citadels,
that you may describe them
    to future generations.
For that is what God is like.
    He is our God forever and ever,
    and he will guide us until we die.

1. *What does it mean to meditate on the love of God? How does one do this?*

2. *What are some ways we can speak about God to the next generation? How can we pass on the faith to our children and grandchildren?*

3. *How does God guide us even at the end of life?*

DAY THREE READING AND QUESTIONS

Psalm 84 (NIV)

How lovely is your dwelling place,
  LORD Almighty!
My soul yearns, even faints,
  for the courts of the LORD;
my heart and my flesh cry out
  for the living God.
Even the sparrow has found a home,
  and the swallow a nest for herself,
  where she may have her young—
a place near your altar,
  LORD Almighty, my King and my God.
Blessed are those who dwell in your house;
  they are ever praising you.
Blessed are those whose strength is in you,
  whose hearts are set on pilgrimage.
As they pass through the Valley of Baka,
  they make it a place of springs;
  the autumn rains also cover it with pools.
They go from strength to strength,
  till each appears before God in Zion.
Hear my prayer, LORD God Almighty;
  listen to me, God of Jacob.
Look on our shield, O God;
  look with favor on your anointed one.

Better is one day in your courts
than a thousand elsewhere;
I would rather be a doorkeeper in the house of my God
than dwell in the tents of the wicked.
For the Lord God is a sun and shield;
the Lord bestows favor and honor;
no good thing does he withhold
from those whose walk is blameless.
Lord Almighty,
blessed is the one who trusts in you.

1. *Do we long to be in the presence of God? How does it feel to be in his presence?*

2. *Where does God live today? What is his temple?*

3. *What is the connection between being blameless and trusting in the Lord?*

DAY FOUR READING AND QUESTIONS

Psalm 122 (NLT)

I was glad when they said to me,
"Let us go to the house of the Lord."
And now here we are,
standing inside your gates, O Jerusalem.
Jerusalem is a well-built city;
its seamless walls cannot be breached.
All the tribes of Israel—the Lord's people—
make their pilgrimage here.
They come to give thanks to the name of the Lord,
as the law requires of Israel.

Here stand the thrones where judgment is given,
    the thrones of the dynasty of David.
Pray for peace in Jerusalem.
    May all who love this city prosper.
O Jerusalem, may there be peace within your walls
    and prosperity in your palaces.
For the sake of my family and friends, I will say,
    "May you have peace."
For the sake of the house of the Lord our God,
    I will seek what is best for you, O Jerusalem.

1. *What is the house of the Lord? Where is it today?*

2. *Do we want to be judged by God? Do we rejoice to approach his throne of judgment?*

3. *Should we pray for the peace of Jerusalem? If so, is this prayer only for the literal city?*

DAY FIVE READING AND QUESTIONS

Go back and read Psalms 48, 84, and 122.

1. *Why might we think of God as especially present on mountains? What feelings come as you think of mountains?*

2. *Have you ever been in a magnificent temple, cathedral, church, or other building? What feelings do those buildings bring to mind?*

3. *What is a pilgrimage? Have you ever been on a pilgrimage? Where did you go? Are we all on a pilgrimage to God's temple?*

Meditation on Psalms 48, 84, and 122

"Where is God?"

Once in a sermon for children, I asked them that question and asked them to point to where God is.

Some pointed upward. God is in heaven above. From there, he rules our world with compassion and justice. And we long for the day when heaven comes to earth and we see God face-to-face.

Some of the children pointed to their hearts. God lives in us. The God who became flesh now lives in us through his Holy Spirit. God is right inside us.

Some pointed in a circle. God is everywhere! There is no corner of our world or in the universe where he cannot be found. God is all around us.

But at one point, when asked where God is, his people would have pointed to Mount Zion in Jerusalem. They would sing these Psalms as they made their pilgrimage to the temple, the place where God lived. Yet even in the early days of the temple, the Israelites knew that it did not contain God. God is everywhere. In every nation. In every city. Yet, in some special way, his glory filled the temple in Jerusalem.

Today we also know that God is everywhere. Yet there are places where we more deeply feel his presence, places of pilgrimage. Think of a place where you have encountered God. Think of the joy that brought. Carry that presence with you today.

"LORD God, no building can contain you. Yet you show yourself to us in many places. May we see you in our hearts. May we know you are all around us. May we someday see you face-to-face."

Consider singing these songs as you continue your meditation: "LORD of All Being, Throned Afar" and "10,000 Reasons."

SALVATION HISTORY PSALMS

Psalms 135 and 136

DAY ONE READING AND QUESTIONS

Psalm 135 (NIV)

Praise the Lord.
Praise the name of the Lord;
    praise him, you servants of the Lord,
you who minister in the house of the Lord,
    in the courts of the house of our God.
Praise the Lord, for the Lord is good;
    sing praise to his name, for that is pleasant.
For the Lord has chosen Jacob to be his own,
    Israel to be his treasured possession.
I know that the Lord is great,
    that our Lord is greater than all gods.
The Lord does whatever pleases him,
    in the heavens and on the earth,
    in the seas and all their depths.
He makes clouds rise from the ends of the earth;
    he sends lightning with the rain
    and brings out the wind from his storehouses.
He struck down the firstborn of Egypt,
    the firstborn of people and animals.
He sent his signs and wonders into your midst, Egypt,
    against Pharaoh and all his servants.
He struck down many nations
    and killed mighty kings—

Sihon king of the Amorites,
    Og king of Bashan,
    and all the kings of Canaan—
and he gave their land as an inheritance,
    an inheritance to his people Israel.

1. *Why did God choose Israel as his possession? Why has God chosen us as his people?*

2. *This Psalm echoes the Exodus story. Why did God deliver Israel from slavery in Egypt? Why is that story still important to us today?*

3. *God struck down nations and kings. How can God's destructive power be good news?*

DAY TWO READING AND QUESTIONS

Psalm 135 (NIV)

Your name, LORD, endures forever,
    your renown, LORD, through all generations.
For the LORD will vindicate his people
    and have compassion on his servants.
The idols of the nations are silver and gold,
    made by human hands.
They have mouths, but cannot speak,
    eyes, but cannot see.
They have ears, but cannot hear,
    nor is there breath in their mouths.
Those who make them will be like them,
    and so will all who trust in them.
All you Israelites, praise the LORD;
    house of Aaron, praise the LORD;

house of Levi, praise the LORD;
  you who fear him, praise the LORD.
Praise be to the LORD from Zion,
  to him who dwells in Jerusalem.
Praise the LORD.

1. *Often the Psalms praise the name of the Lord. Are names important in our culture? Why is the name of the Lord important? Do we even think of God having a name?*

2. *Those who worship idols become like idols. Do we become like what we worship? What are some idols in our culture?*

3. *What is the significance of Aaron and Levi praising God? Do we have priests today? How do they praise God?*

DAY THREE READING AND QUESTIONS

Psalm 136 (NLT)

Give thanks to the LORD, for he is good!
  His faithful love endures forever.
Give thanks to the God of gods.
  His faithful love endures forever.
Give thanks to the LORD of lords.
  His faithful love endures forever.
Give thanks to him who alone does mighty miracles.
  His faithful love endures forever.
Give thanks to him who made the heavens so skillfully.
  His faithful love endures forever.
Give thanks to him who placed the earth among the waters.
  His faithful love endures forever.

Give thanks to him who made the heavenly lights—
His faithful love endures forever.
the sun to rule the day,
His faithful love endures forever.
and the moon and stars to rule the night.
His faithful love endures forever.
Give thanks to him who killed the firstborn of Egypt.
His faithful love endures forever.
He brought Israel out of Egypt.
His faithful love endures forever.
He acted with a strong hand and powerful arm.
His faithful love endures forever.

1. *This Psalm goes back to the creation story in Genesis. Why should we praise God for creation? How does creation show his enduring love?*

2. *God made the great lights—the sun, moon, and stars. What is the importance of light? What other kind of light is spoken of in the Bible?*

3. *This Psalm also talks of the first Passover, when God struck down the firstborn of the Egyptians. Why is Passover important to us? What should we remember about Passover?*

DAY FOUR READING AND QUESTIONS

Psalm 136 (NLT)

Give thanks to him who parted the Red Sea.
His faithful love endures forever.
He led Israel safely through,
His faithful love endures forever.
but he hurled Pharaoh and his army into the Red Sea.
His faithful love endures forever.

Give thanks to him who led his people through the wilderness.
His faithful love endures forever.
Give thanks to him who struck down mighty kings.
His faithful love endures forever.
He killed powerful kings—
His faithful love endures forever.
Sihon king of the Amorites,
His faithful love endures forever.
and Og king of Bashan.
His faithful love endures forever.
God gave the land of these kings as an inheritance—
His faithful love endures forever.
a special possession to his servant Israel.
His faithful love endures forever.
He remembered us in our weakness.
His faithful love endures forever.
He saved us from our enemies.
His faithful love endures forever.
He gives food to every living thing.
His faithful love endures forever.
Give thanks to the God of heaven.
His faithful love endures forever.

1. *Why is the Red Sea story so amazing? What does it tell us about God's love?*

2. *How has God freed us from our enemies?*

3. *Do we depend on God for food? Why do we sometimes take this for granted?*

DAY FIVE READING AND QUESTIONS

Go back and read Psalms 135 and 136.

1. *What is the value of history? Why is it that we can more clearly see the work of God in the past than in the present?*

2. *It may be hard for us to relate to these stories of what God has done for Israel in the past. Think of stories from your own past. Where have you seen the loving and powerful acts of God?*

3. *Psalm 136 has a refrain, "His faithful love endures forever." Do we believe this? When is it hard to believe this? Does remembering what God has done in the past help us believe? How?*

Meditation on Psalms 135 and 136

Do you remember Michael Jackson's "moonwalk"? In that dance move, he looked as if he was walking forward when he was actually going backward.

We moonwalk with God. That is, we walk backward into the future. We cannot see the future behind us, but as we moonwalk backward into the future, our face is toward the past. In the same way, we cannot see what God will do in the future, but we can see what he has done for us in the past.

This is why history is so important—not as the trivial pursuit of ancient times but as the way we see God's loving hand in the past. He has made us, fed us, protected us, healed us, and led us. Because we remember his past acts of love, we trust that his love is still with us in the present and will be with us in the future. His love endures forever.

These Psalms show us how to look back at what God has done for us and our ancestors so we can believe he will sustain us in the present. We need that faith particularly when times are tough. No matter how it looks now, God's love endures forever.

"God of love, may we constantly remember how you led us kindly in the past so we might trust you now and in the future. Increase our faith!"

Consider singing these songs as you continue your meditation: "O How Kindly Hast Thou Led Me" and "I Will Remember You."

WISDOM PSALMS

Psalm 37

DAY ONE READING AND QUESTIONS

Psalm 37 (NIV)

Do not fret because of those who are evil
  or be envious of those who do wrong;
for like the grass they will soon wither,
  like green plants they will soon die away.
Trust in the LORD and do good;
  dwell in the land and enjoy safe pasture.
Take delight in the LORD,
  and he will give you the desires of your heart.
Commit your way to the LORD;
  trust in him and he will do this:
He will make your righteous reward shine like the dawn,
  your vindication like the noonday sun.
Be still before the LORD
  and wait patiently for him;
do not fret when people succeed in their ways,
  when they carry out their wicked schemes.
Refrain from anger and turn from wrath;
  do not fret—it leads only to evil.
For those who are evil will be destroyed,
  but those who hope in the LORD will inherit the land.

1. *Why do those who cheat and harm others sometimes grow rich and prosper? Is this right? How does that make you feel? What will happen to such people?*

2. *God will give us the desires of our hearts. Does this mean God will give us anything we want? If not, what does it really mean?*

3. *What does it mean to be still before God? Why must we wait patiently for God?*

DAY TWO READING AND QUESTIONS

Psalm 37 (NIV)

A little while, and the wicked will be no more;
  though you look for them, they will not be found.
But the meek will inherit the land
  and enjoy peace and prosperity.
The wicked plot against the righteous
  and gnash their teeth at them;
but the LORD laughs at the wicked,
  for he knows their day is coming.
The wicked draw the sword
  and bend the bow
to bring down the poor and needy,
  to slay those whose ways are upright.
But their swords will pierce their own hearts,
  and their bows will be broken.
Better the little that the righteous have
  than the wealth of many wicked;
for the power of the wicked will be broken,
  but the LORD upholds the righteous.
The blameless spend their days under the LORD's care,
  and their inheritance will endure forever.
In times of disaster they will not wither;
  in days of famine they will enjoy plenty.

1. *What comes to mind when you think of "wicked"? How are the wicked described in this Psalm? Do we often associate wickedness with violence?*

2. *What does it mean to be meek? How will the meek inherit the land?*

3. *Here God laughs at the wicked. What kind of laughter is this? Do you ever think of God laughing in this way?*

DAY THREE READING AND QUESTIONS

Psalm 37 (NIV)

But the wicked will perish:
 Though the LORD's enemies are like the flowers of the field,
 they will be consumed, they will go up in smoke.
The wicked borrow and do not repay,
 but the righteous give generously;
those the LORD blesses will inherit the land,
 but those he curses will be destroyed.
The LORD makes firm the steps
 of the one who delights in him;
though he may stumble, he will not fall,
 for the LORD upholds him with his hand.
I was young and now I am old,
 yet I have never seen the righteous forsaken
 or their children begging bread.
They are always generous and lend freely;
 their children will be a blessing.
Turn from evil and do good;
 then you will dwell in the land forever.
For the LORD loves the just
 and will not forsake his faithful ones.

Wrongdoers will be completely destroyed;
the offspring of the wicked will perish.
The righteous will inherit the land
and dwell in it forever.
The mouths of the righteous utter wisdom,
and their tongues speak what is just.
The law of their God is in their hearts;
their feet do not slip.

1. *How does the way we handle money make us wicked or righteous?*

2. *The Psalmist says he has never seen the righteous forsaken or their children begging for bread. Has that been your experience?*

3. *How does our speech show we are righteous? What is the relationship between speech and having the law in our hearts?*

DAY FOUR READING AND QUESTIONS

Psalm 37 (NIV)

The wicked lie in wait for the righteous,
intent on putting them to death;
but the LORD will not leave them in the power of the wicked
or let them be condemned when brought to trial.
Hope in the LORD
and keep his way.
He will exalt you to inherit the land;
when the wicked are destroyed, you will see it.
I have seen a wicked and ruthless man
flourishing like a luxuriant native tree,
but he soon passed away and was no more;
though I looked for him, he could not be found.

Consider the blameless, observe the upright;
 a future awaits those who seek peace.
But all sinners will be destroyed;
 there will be no future for the wicked.
The salvation of the righteous comes from the Lord;
 he is their stronghold in time of trouble.
The Lord helps them and delivers them;
 he delivers them from the wicked and saves them,
 because they take refuge in him.

1. *The Lord defends the righteous when the wicked bring them to trial. How does the fairness of our justice system reflect wickedness or righteousness?*

2. *There is no future for the wicked. Is this true? Proverbially true? Should we take comfort in this?*

3. *By contrast, the future belongs to those who seek peace. How do we seek peace? How does this relate to trusting God as our stronghold?*

DAY FIVE READING AND QUESTIONS

Go back and read Psalm 37.

1. *This Psalm is similar to the book of Proverbs. What is a proverb? Can you find proverbs in this Psalm?*

2. *What is the relationship between wisdom and justice in this Psalm? Do we sometimes mistakenly think the wise thing to do is to ignore injustice? Does God ignore injustice?*

3. *Who also said, "Blessed are the peacemakers" and "The meek shall inherit the earth"?*

Meditation on Psalm 37

The wicked versus the righteous.

These words—"wicked" and "righteous"—sometimes carry the opposite meaning of how they are used in the Bible. In contemporary slang, "wicked" can mean "outstanding" or "excellent," as in "That's a wicked car" or "The pitcher has a wicked curveball."

"Righteous" has also changed its meaning. Most people cannot hear "righteous" without thinking "self-righteous." The word "righteous" implies narrow-mindedly condemning everyone we see. You wouldn't want to overhear your friends calling you "righteous," as in "She thinks she's so righteous."

But in the Bible, as in this Psalm, the righteous are those who trust in the Lord and who show it by giving to the poor, seeking peace, controlling their anger, and speaking the truth. By contrast, the wicked use their power to cheat, attack, and even kill the poor and needy.

The righteous win. The wicked lose. That is the message of this Psalm.

But it doesn't always seem that way. It looks as if the rich get richer at the expense of the poor. The rich control the government. The rich win court cases. The poor lose again and again.

Yet we are called to trust in the Lord. This Psalm says to wait patiently and God will make things right. Justice will prevail. The wicked will wither and die. The meek will inherit the earth. Yes, we work for justice, but we trust God to work. We do not put our faith in human schemes to make the world right.

"God of the poor and righteous, increase our trust in you! May the day of justice come soon."

Consider singing these songs as you continue your meditation: "God of Justice" and "We Are Called to Be God's People."

SONGS OF TRUST

Psalms 27, 62, 63, and 131

DAY ONE READING AND QUESTIONS

Psalm 27 (NLT)

The LORD is my light and my salvation—
so why should I be afraid?
The LORD is my fortress, protecting me from danger,
so why should I tremble?
When evil people come to devour me,
when my enemies and foes attack me,
they will stumble and fall.
Though a mighty army surrounds me,
my heart will not be afraid.
Even if I am attacked,
I will remain confident.
The one thing I ask of the LORD—
the thing I seek most—
is to live in the house of the LORD all the days of my life,
delighting in the LORD's perfections
and meditating in his Temple.
For he will conceal me there when troubles come;
he will hide me in his sanctuary.
He will place me out of reach on a high rock.
Then I will hold my head high
above my enemies who surround me.
At his sanctuary I will offer sacrifices with shouts of joy,
singing and praising the LORD with music.
Hear me as I pray, O LORD.
Be merciful and answer me!

1. *What are you afraid of? List those fears. How does the Lord take away those fears?*

2. *Do you think of God as beautiful? Do you long to gaze upon the beauty of God? What does that mean?*

3. *What causes joy, singing, and music in this Psalm? Does it cause those things in your life?*

DAY TWO READING AND QUESTIONS

Psalm 27 (NLT)

My heart has heard you say, "Come and talk with me."
    And my heart responds, "LORD, I am coming."
Do not turn your back on me.
    Do not reject your servant in anger.
    You have always been my helper.
Don't leave me now; don't abandon me,
    O God of my salvation!
Even if my father and mother abandon me,
    the LORD will hold me close.
Teach me how to live, O LORD.
    Lead me along the right path,
    for my enemies are waiting for me.
Do not let me fall into their hands.
    For they accuse me of things I've never done;
    with every breath they threaten me with violence.
Yet I am confident I will see the LORD's goodness
    while I am here in the land of the living.
Wait patiently for the LORD.
    Be brave and courageous.
    Yes, wait patiently for the LORD.

1. *What does it mean to talk to God?*

2. *Have you ever been (or felt) forsaken by your parents? Can you imagine how that would feel? How does that feeling contrast with our trust in God?*

3. *Why must we wait for the Lord? How do we wait? Do you find it difficult to wait?*

DAY THREE READING AND QUESTIONS

Psalm 62 (NIV)

Truly my soul finds rest in God;
  my salvation comes from him.
Truly he is my rock and my salvation;
  he is my fortress, I will never be shaken.
How long will you assault me?
  Would all of you throw me down—
  this leaning wall, this tottering fence?
Surely they intend to topple me
  from my lofty place;
  they take delight in lies.
With their mouths they bless,
  but in their hearts they curse.
Yes, my soul, find rest in God;
  my hope comes from him.
Truly he is my rock and my salvation;
  he is my fortress, I will not be shaken.
My salvation and my honor depend on God;
  he is my mighty rock, my refuge.

Trust in him at all times, you people;
 pour out your hearts to him,
 for God is our refuge.
Surely the lowborn are but a breath,
 the highborn are but a lie.
If weighed on a balance, they are nothing;
 together they are only a breath.
Do not trust in extortion
 or put vain hope in stolen goods;
though your riches increase,
 do not set your heart on them.
One thing God has spoken,
 two things I have heard:
"Power belongs to you, God,
 and with you, LORD, is unfailing love";
and, "You reward everyone
 according to what they have done."

1. *What does it mean to rest in God? How do we rest in him? Do you find it difficult to rest? If so, why?*

2. *Do people ever try to tear you down? Who can we go to in order to be built up?*

3. *The Lord rewards everyone according to what they have done. Is this good news or bad news?*

DAY FOUR READING AND QUESTIONS

Psalm 63 (NLT)

O God, you are my God;
 I earnestly search for you.

My soul thirsts for you;
    my whole body longs for you
in this parched and weary land
    where there is no water.
I have seen you in your sanctuary
    and gazed upon your power and glory.
Your unfailing love is better than life itself;
    how I praise you!
I will praise you as long as I live,
    lifting up my hands to you in prayer.
You satisfy me more than the richest feast.
    I will praise you with songs of joy.
I lie awake thinking of you,
    meditating on you through the night.
Because you are my helper,
    I sing for joy in the shadow of your wings.
I cling to you;
    your strong right hand holds me securely.
But those plotting to destroy me will come to ruin.
    They will go down into the depths of the earth.
They will die by the sword
    and become the food of jackals.
But the king will rejoice in God.
    All who swear to tell the truth will praise him,
    while liars will be silenced.

Psalm 131 (NIV)

My heart is not proud, LORD,
    my eyes are not haughty;
I do not concern myself with great matters
    or things too wonderful for me.

But I have calmed and quieted myself,
    I am like a weaned child with its mother;
    like a weaned child I am content.
Israel, put your hope in the Lord
    both now and forevermore.

1. *Think of a time when you felt thirsty or hungry. Do we thirst and hunger for God? How does that feel?*

2. *At night when you cannot sleep, do you think about God?*

3. *Do you calmly trust God about things you cannot understand or control? How is that like a child trusting in his or her mother?*

DAY FIVE READING AND QUESTIONS

Go back and read Psalms 27, 62, 63, and 131.

1. *Do you ever feel like hiding from others? How does the Lord hide us?*

2. *Can you remember what it was like to rest in the arms of your mother? Describe that feeling. How is our relationship with God like that?*

3. *Do we spend too much time trying to figure out things that are beyond us? Can we admit that there is more and more that we do not understand?*

Meditation on Psalms 27, 62, 63, and 131

God is our Father. And in Psalm 131, God is a loving Mother with a baby in her arms.

This takes me back to my childhood. I had good and loving parents who provided for me. I rarely remember being afraid, because I knew Dad and Mom were there. In those few moments when I was afraid (as with nightmares of the big, bad wolf), Mom would come into my room, take me in her arms, and all was well.

The same is true with God in these Psalms. He is the one who protects us from harm—our rock, shelter, and sanctuary.

When I was a kid, I never went hungry or thirsty. When I was hungry, Mom would bring food. When I was thirsty, even in the middle of the night, Mom or Dad would bring a glass of water. I never worried about food as a child.

The Lord provides us with drink and food. What is more, he teaches us to hunger and thirst for him. It is God alone who satisfies our deepest hunger.

When I was a kid, I didn't realize I trusted my parents. I just did. I took their provision, protection, and love for granted. They were just there.

So it is with our God. He is faithful and dependable. His love is ever with us. Even when times are darkest and the nightmares come, God folds us in motherly arms. So we do not try to understand why things happen, things too wonderful for us to even imagine, we rest in the arms of our Mother.

Perhaps you did not have loving parents. But surely you can imagine what that would have been like—and thus you can envision the loving arms of your Mother and Father. What God asks of us is to be his children. Let him take care of us. Stop striving to be in control and have all the answers. Play in the courts of the Lord. Long to see God's face.

"Loving Mother, hold us close to you. We long to see your face. We thirst for you."

Consider singing these songs as you continue your meditation: "Dear Lord and Father of Mankind" and "Come to the Quiet."

Twelve Volumes Covering the New Testament

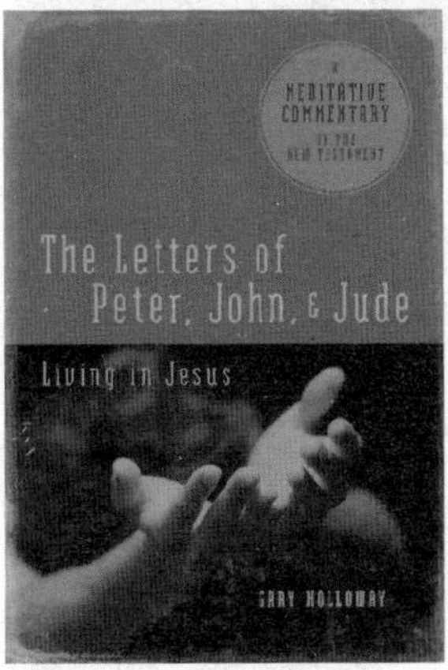

Hebrews & James
by Gary Holloway
ISBN 978-0-89112-505-1

John
by Gary Holloway
ISBN 978-0-89112-504-4

Mark
by Earl Lavender
ISBN 978-0-89112-551-8

The Letters of Peter, John, & Jude
by Gary Holloway
ISBN 978-0-89112-557-0

Revelation
by Terry Briley
ISBN 978-0-89112-559-4

Do you want a deeper, more fulfilling way of Bible study? Do you want to know God through Scripture—not just to know the teachings but to have a relationship with the Teacher? This meditative commentary is for you. There are many commentaries on the books of the Bible, but this series is different. It employs the classic Christian method of "holy reading" to help you hear the voice of God.

Holy reading involves slowly engaging a short passage of Scripture, listening closely, reading repeatedly, praying the words, and perhaps sharing with fellow believers. God will bless us, our families, and our churches if we take the time to be still, listen, and do his word.

www.leafwoodpublishers.com

Also from Gary Holloway

LIVING GOD'S LOVE

An Invitation to Christian Spirituality

ISBN 9780974844121

A life richer than you can imagine

Do you want a deeper relationship with God? A closer walk with Jesus? A sense of the Holy Spirit's constant presence? Is this the deepest desire of your heart, but you don't know where to begin? This book is for you. It offers no shortcuts or sure-fire techniques for a deeper spirituality. But it serves as a simple and easy-to-follow signpost marking the path of daily relationship with God.

God invites you into relationship with him, just as you are. Even if you're not sure about God, even if you have no religious background, even if you've been a churchgoer all your life, God invites you to share his very life. It is a life richer than you can imagine.

"*At last: a book that brings the essential subject of spiritual formation down to earth. Clear, reverent, practical, and warm.*"

—**Brian McLaren,** author of *A Generous Orthodoxy* and *Faith after Doubt*

"*This profoundly simple book grounds the practices of spiritual maturing in a sound theology of relation in and with God. The result is not a simple formula for instant spirituality but healthy food for the soul.*"

—**Randy Harris,** author of *Living Jesus* and *Daring Faith*

1-877-816-4455 toll free
www.leafwoodpublishers.com

LEAFWOOD PUBLISHERS
an imprint of Abilene Christian University Press